# A WARLESS WORLD

# A
# WARLESS
# WORLD

EDITED BY
*Arthur Larson*

*McGraw-Hill Book Company, Inc.*

NEW YORK   TORONTO   LONDON

117956

# Acknowledgments

The editor wishes to express his thanks for the generous grant from the Johnson Foundation (Racine, Wisconsin, Leslie Paffrath, president) which made preparation of this book possible. Thanks are also due to the *Saturday Review,* which has published portions of this book from time to time; to its editor, Norman Cousins, who was active in the initiation and execution of the project; to Harry Hollins, who was helpful in the planning stage; and to Mary Kersey Harvey, who has played a vital part in all aspects of the venture from beginning to end.

*Arthur Larson*

Durham, North Carolina
July, 1963

# Contents

# Foreword

It gives me much satisfaction, in response to Mr. Arthur Larson's request, to contribute a brief foreword to this symposium.

The basic assumption of the volume—a warless world—is in line with the primary objective of the United Nations. The preamble of the Charter speaks of the determination of the peoples of the world to save succeeding generations from the scourge of war. Almost every day I receive numerous communications, from individuals as well as organizations throughout the world, voicing their hopes and fears—their hopes for a warless world and their fears for human survival in the nuclear age. Their anxiety and desire for communication is understandable because, while the United Nations is an intergovernmental organization, it exists for the peoples of the world as much as for the governments who are its Member States.

Many books and studies have recently been published in which writers and contributors assume, not a warless world, but one in which scientific achievements would continue to be integrated into the military system—the system of the nuclear deterrent, with its precarious balance of terror, upon which the maintenance of peace is believed to depend. However, in the face of the serious risks that this traditional concept entails, responsible people in and out of authority, statesmen as well as serious students, have come increasingly to envisage a warless world—a world which has voluntarily divested itself of weapons of mass destruction—as being not only a necessary, but even a realistic goal.

The present activities of the United Nations—to keep the peace, to facilitate peaceful change, to promote social progress and better standards of life and larger freedom—all point in the same direction. Our activities are the first steps—often groping, certainly incomplete—toward the kind of effective international authority which is necessary to keep the peace in a warless world.

I believe that there will be common ground that eventually there should be an international authority which is generally acceptable to all nations, large and small, and which is compatible with all rational social systems. Every step in the direction of conciliation of existing political differences, every attempt to reconcile the clash of ideologies, every practical agreement designed to solve a current problem will have, at the same time, the effect of strengthening the authority of the United Nations and the world community.

From this point of view I welcome this symposium as an intellectual exercise exploring, and to some extent dispelling the fear of, the unknown. Mr. Larson has obviously made every effort to secure the utmost objectivity, and has also included an appendix in regard to "Our Idea of a World without Arms," as seen from the point of view of the Soviet Union. Even so, it is inevitable that he and his distinguished fellow-contributors, coming as they do from the Western world, should see the problem from their own angle; and it is not possible for me, nor would it be expected of me, to subscribe to all their ideas and views. It is my belief, however, that such exercises serve a very valuable purpose. They deal not with a Utopian concept but with a practical goal.

I hope that this problem of the institutional as well as the psychological and other changes and adjustments that are essential to bring a warless world into existence will be studied from different angles, and that similar exercises will be undertaken by more and more individuals and organizations the world over, so that out of a continuing study of this problem a consensus might emerge pointing the way to a future without fear.

U THANT

26 July 1963

# Introduction

This book—despite its visionary-sounding title—is an effort to deal in a practical way with a number of issues relevant to the success of current disarmament negotiations. The technique adopted (a technique dear to mathematicians, as Jules Moch points out) is to "assume the problem solved," that is, to assume the success of the disarmament negotiations and then to take a hard look at the kind of world we would have. Would we really like such a world? Could we keep it even if we got it started? What would be the effect on national security, on the processes of change and revolution, on the struggle of values and ideologies, on economic development or disruption, on the population problem, and on the moral, psychological and spiritual state of mankind?

An immediate reason for applying this technique to the disarmament question is that progress in disarmament negotiation is undoubtedly being impeded by subconscious and unspoken fears of the risks thought to attend the dismantling of weapons systems. The fear of depression and unemployment is the only one that has had much study or discussion. Among the stronger, better established nations, the fear of insecurity may loom even larger. Among the newly developing countries, and among progressive-minded people everywhere, a quite different fear may predominate: the fear that the *status quo* may be crystallized and desirable change thus prevented. In addition, there may be in many minds a secret fear that the ideas and values of one's particular culture would lose out against those of competing cultures and ideologies, if not backed by armaments. Such thoughts are often felt to be so shameful that they are kept suppressed in the subregions of the collective consciousness, where they nevertheless continue to influence public attitudes and national policy. This book can help to drag some of these hidden fears out into the daylight where they can be properly studied and appraised.

The other principal purpose is to analyze and present the variety and extent of the positive benefits of all kinds—not merely material—that would flow from disarmament under law. This has never been attempted in adequate detail, perhaps because of the fear of seeming Utopian. Consequently, there has never been a chance to have the incentive for progress in negotiations that would come from a full weighing of risks against gains.

The contributors to this volume all began with a common set of assumptions. (The fact that a writer has participated in this analysis does not, however, mean that he believes that the conditions postulated are probable or even possible.)

The assumptions are: that disarmament has been achieved under an agreement entered into voluntarily and in good faith by all states whose participation would be necessary to make such an arrangement effective; that disarmament in this sense is taken to be a condition in which national arms have been reduced to the level of police forces necessary to keep internal order, and in which there is an internationally administered armed force stronger than any combination of national forces that might be aligned against it; and that disarmament has been accompanied by the creation of a peace-keeping and dispute-settling system with at least the minimal amount of law and organization necessary to prevent large-scale organized armed conflict among states.

These assumptions, far from being fanciful, are an almost literal transcription of official policy. Beginning with the speech of Secretary of State Herter to the National Press Club in February, 1960, continuing through President Kennedy's United Nations speech of September 25, 1961, and culminating in the detailed American disarmament proposals of April, 1962, runs this theme: As we tear down armaments toward the ultimate level of general and complete disarmament, we must build up peace-keeping machinery to take their place, until eventually the peace is kept by a system of international tribunals backed by an unchallengeable international force.

In the analysis based on these assumptions, four divisions will be discernible. These reflect the thought that there are four main needs that must be affirmatively served by a world without war: security, change, material well-being and progress, and spiritual, moral, and psychological well-being and progress. This pattern corresponds to the four principal fears mentioned earlier: the fear, especially in the stronger countries, that safety might be weakened; the fear, principally in newer countries, that change might be blocked; the fear that disarmament might cause economic hardship; and the fear that the ideals of one's culture might not survive without arms backing.

There was no effort to prejudge the tone or the findings that would emerge from the thinking that went into these chapters. The two-way theme of "problems and opportunities" called for presenting the rough with the smooth, and there was no presumption that any particular line of inquiry must always lead to a happy ending. It is hoped that the combination of knowledge, experience in public life, and intellectual ingenuity brought to bear by the authors upon the unprecedented difficulties and opportunities suggested by the stated assumptions will leave the reader with some useful fresh lines of thought on the world's most pressing problem.

# I

## Keeping peace in a world without arms

BY LOUIS B. SOHN

Bemis Professor of International Law,
Harvard Law School

Our view of the world of the future is distorted by two contradictory fears. We are afraid, in the first place, that in a disarmed world the present order, however precarious, will be replaced by anarchy. If the threat of nuclear war should no longer hang over the world, other kinds of hostility might increase markedly. Indirect aggression and subversion, fomented by unscrupulous neighbors, might destroy the established governments in many countries, and a deadly struggle between capitalism and communism would break out in a hundred places. Is this the kind of peace and security that we can expect in a disarmed world?

In the second place, a world without war conjures a vision of a static world, where change could no longer be brought about by violence. Nations would remain forever bound by the accidental boundaries of today and there would be no way to break out of intolerable situations imposed by the dead hand of the past. A world like that does not seem possible to us who are faced every day with revolutionary changes in the political, social, and economic fabric throughout the globe. Can a way be found to maintain peace and ensure change at the same time?

Faced with these dilemmas, we sometimes wonder whether we really want disarmament. But a close study of the problem shows that if we want to increase national security, there is no other choice. Even most military men agree that neither side in the present struggle can improve its security by piling new armaments on top of the old ones, if the other side does the same. Regardless of any additions to the Western panoply of weapons, the simultaneous increase in the Soviet means of attack, even if smaller than that of the West, makes the security of the West more precarious every year. With the passage of time, more and more horrible weapons are at the disposal of a potential attacker, and the danger of total destruction increases proportionally. It will be of little satisfaction to a victim of an attack that the enemy will also be destroyed by a retaliatory blow. National-security forces have been built to deter an attack, and the better prepared they are the less likely an attack will be; but once an attack comes, reciprocal ruin will be the only result. There is only one way out of this impasse—a reversal of the arms race, a gradual reduction of national military forces, under effective international control, down to the point where they no longer will threaten mutual annihilation.

But mere abolition of nuclear weapons and of means for delivering them on target will not abolish the danger of nuclear destruction. If nations retain sufficient arms to wage a limited war, any such war can easily grow into a nuclear war, for the losing side is likely to be tempted to utilize newly built nuclear weapons to turn the tide to its advantage. Even in a completely disarmed world, a nation could use its remaining police force for an attack on an unprepared rival. Great havoc was brought about throughout some 3,000 years of recorded history by primitive weapons; it is enough to remember Rome's destruction of Carthage, the conquests of Attila and his Huns and of Genghis Khan and his Mongol warriors, and the quick spread of Mohammedanism from Arabia to the area stretching from India to Spain. The present situation is complicated by the fact that knowledge of the new weapons cannot be obliterated and if a war should start, arms production would be revived and nuclear weapons would be brought back. It is not sufficient, therefore, to devise methods for reducing arms and for verifying that nations have actually disarmed. Parallel steps must be taken in other areas to strengthen the institutions for keeping the peace.

There is another factor to be taken into account. No inspection system is foolproof, and a determined aggressor can secret a sizable amount of dangerous weapons without risk of immediate detection. This need not lead to the conclusion that disarmament is impossible, but means other than deterrent national forces must be found to deal severely with an aggressor or, even better, to stop him at the first sign of danger. We know now that Hitler could easily have been stopped in the early stages of his career, and that his generals would have deserted him if his bluff had been called when the German army marched into the Rhineland in violation of the Treaty of Versailles. A concerted action at the right time and place may require only a small amount of force, but each delay increases the risk that large-scale warfare would be necessary to stop the designs of an aggressor growing more bold with each unrebuffed success.

We have seen in Egypt and the Congo that peace can be restored by a small international force having the backing of world public opinion. We know that such a force even today can prevent small wars in which none of the Great Powers are seriously involved; and it can police areas of potential danger such as the boundary between Israel and the United Arab Republic. But at present we cannot conceive of a force strong enough to deal with the principal threat to peace—the constantly growing armaments of the Great Powers. Only after a considerable measure of disarmament, will it be possible to rely on an international force as a real guarantee against war from any quarter. It is in this spirit that the Joint Statement of Agreed Principles, issued by the United States and the Soviet Union on September 20, 1961, provided for the establishment during the final stages of disarmament of "an international police force to be equipped with agreed types of armaments" and strong enough to "ensure that the United Nations can effectively deter or suppress any threat or use of arms" in violation of the United Nations Charter.

There seems to be, therefore, a general agreement that international peace and security in a disarmed world will be maintained by an international peace force. To accomplish this goal, such a force will have to be truly international, highly mobile, and able to decide quickly that action is necessary. At the same time, safeguards must be developed against possible abuse of the force and against its possible domination by a particular group of nations or a modern Caesar.

In the first place, such a force is likely to be composed of highly trained, hand-picked, and well-paid volunteers rather than national contingents commanded by national officers following the orders of their home governments. Some of the experiences in the Congo show the danger of national contingents with divided loyalty, which are more likely to obey their own authorities instead of the United Nations commanders. If the service in the United Nations forces is made sufficiently attractive, with special benefits during the service and after its termination, there will be no dearth of volunteers. The most suitable individuals can be picked from the many candidates through rigorous testing of their qualifications and attitudes, and methods can be devised to ensure that the chosen individuals will be internationally minded rather than nationalistic.

To safeguard against domination by any national group, it may be necessary to limit the percentage of nationals of any nation in the force as a whole, in the various services, and in the officer corps. Similarly, limits may be imposed on the participation of nations from certain groups of nations bound by an alliance, such as NATO or the Warsaw Pact. Units of the force should be composed, to the greatest possible extent, of nationals of different nations, and even the command of small units of persons of the same national origin ought to be in the hands of officers of different nationality.

There should be the maximum possible amount of dispersal of the force throughout the world. The units of the force need to be stationed in such a fashion that they will be able to reach any danger spot quickly. They must be so strong that they cannot be overpowered easily by any nation or group of nations. For these reasons they ought to be located in the territory of small nations, and their main bases may be put on easily defensible islands or peninsulas. They may be located, for instance, in such places as Trinidad, Madeira, Iceland, Malta, Cyprus, Zanzibar, and Ceylon. Only a limited percentage of the force would be stationed in any region, and for this purpose the world would be divided into at least fifteen regions. It may be possible to provide that no less than 5 or more than 10 per cent of the total strength of the force be stationed in any one of these fifteen regions, and that there should be frequent rotation between the regions.

The danger of Caesar worship may be avoided if the command of the force is entrusted, not to a single person, but to a committee of five or seven persons, all of whom preferably ought to be nationals of small nations. At the same time, to ensure the impartiality of decisions, the majority of the command group should come from the noncommitted nations rather than the two major blocs. The military command would be under the constant supervision of a civilian body, such as the standing committee of the United Nations General Assembly, with broad powers of investigation and interrogation. The selection of higher officers of the force and control over the promotion system also ought to be in civilian hands. If the force is authorized to have nuclear weapons to deter their use by any nation possessing a secret stockpile of such weapons, the nuclear weapons must be under strict civilian control, much stronger than the one exercised by the Atomic Energy Commission in the United States. Only if their use has been authorized by the General Assembly would these weapons be transferred from civilian control to the force, and even then their use would be permitted only if the aggressor had actually used nuclear weapons or if he were about to use them.

In general, the force would concentrate on preventive action rather than suppression of acts of international violence. If the force were able to step quickly into any situation likely to endanger peace, its very presence would prevent the aggravation of the situation, might make it easier for the parties to withdraw without losing face, and would provide a cooling-off period. It may be expected that in most situations no actual display of force would be required; even where hostilities had started, the force would not usually join one of the belligerents, but would first attempt to separate them and to establish a neutral zone between the contending parties.

Crucial to this approach would be the existence of effective means of information about any possible threat to the peace. This may be provided through an extension of the current practice of establishing a United Nations "presence" in danger spots around the world. It may be possible to establish United Nations observation posts in the territory of each nation. The number of observers in each country may vary in proportion to the size of each national territory and the likelihood of a conflict with a neighboring nation. If a particular observer group had sufficient reason to believe that a military action was imminent, either by the country in which it is stationed or against that country, it would immediately notify the command of the force and request that a contingent be deployed in the threatened area. Unless the command of the force had strong evidence to the contrary, it would promptly despatch the necessary troops to the trouble spot. Similarly, if there should be an armed attack by one nation against another, the command would be notified about it by the two observer groups in the nations involved in the attack. The command would then request the two parties to the conflict to cease hostilities forthwith and would be ready to step in between them the moment the fighting stopped. Only if both, or one, of the belligerents should make it impossible for the force to establish a neutral zone between the two armies, would it be necessary to have recourse to a political body for a decision as to further action to be taken.

In any case, arrangements must be made to transmit simultaneously to the competent political body each request for action by the force—for example, to the General Assembly of the United Nations, either as constituted at present or suitably modified to cope with its new functions. If such a body should not be in session, it would be called together promptly. Its decisions, approving the use of the force, ordering the cessation of such use, or requesting more drastic action, would require a high majority—but should not be subject to a veto by any nation. If a considerable minority disagreed with a decision, it might appeal to an international tribunal for an injunction, but until such injunction was granted there should be no stoppage in any action needed to maintain peace. The tribunal would investigate the facts of the situation and check whether all procedural and substantive safeguards against an unauthorized use of the international peace force had been complied with. Should the tribunal find that there was no sufficient basis for the use of the force, it would issue an injunction against further use, might order the withdrawal of the force, and might even request that the United Nations pay compensation to the injured nation if the international force caused considerable damage through unauthorized action.

Of course, one can easily imagine other methods of control over the use of an international force, and careful provisions on the subject must be embodied in the treaty establishing the force. Such a force might be established first on a regional basis; later the regional contingents might be welded into a single international peace force.

Assuming that an international peace force could be established and that it would be effective in preventing war between nations, would this automatically establish a peaceful world? There are nations, of course, which are completely satisfied with the present *status quo* and would prefer to have it maintained forever, if necessary through the use of the international peace force. But as Arnold Toynbee points out, an attempt to freeze a situation is apt to have the opposite effect to what is intended. An effective prohibition of the use of force in international relations will deprive nations of their principal remedy in the past against real or alleged violations of their rights and interests. If force can no longer be used to achieve national aims, other remedies must be provided for satisfying just grievances which one nation may have against another. At present, only a minority of the nations of the world have accepted the jurisdiction of the International Court of Justice, and even some of these nations made their acceptance subject to crippling reservations. In addition, there is no parallel body which could render a binding decision in a nonlegal dispute which cannot be submitted to the Court.

It may be assumed that, in a disarmed world, states are going to accept without reservations the jurisdiction of the International Court of Justice to deal with legal disputes between them. In particular, it may be hoped that by that time the United States may find it possible to abandon the Connally reservation excepting from the jurisdiction of the Court all disputes which, as determined unilaterally by the United States, fall within its domestic jurisdiction. The Court, despite the limited number of cases submitted to it, has done an excellent job, and one can look without hesitation to an expansion of its sphere of activity.

Theoretically, all disputes can be decided by a court on the basis of law, and a party presenting a claim not based on law simply will lose its case. Nevertheless, there are disputes which are not suitable for submission to the Court. Usually labeled "political disputes," these do not involve an interpretation of a rule of international law, but a departure from such a rule or a change in a legal situation which a party finds no longer tolerable. Disputes of this type cannot be settled effectively on the basis of existing law, and in the United Nations they are usually dealt with by the General Assembly or the Security Council. But these bodies can only make recommendations, and such recommendations usually relate to procedure rather than substance. In most cases, they limit themselves to a call upon the parties to the dispute to continue negotiations or to an appointment of a mediator. It is generally recognized that neither the Security Council, which is hampered by the veto, nor the unwieldy General Assembly, acting through committees of more than a hundred members, is suitable for dealing objectively with the merits of a dispute. Only an organ removed from daily political controversies and free from the temptation of arriving at final decisions through political deals between various blocs can be trusted with finding a solution which will be unbiased and equitable, and thus acceptable to all nations concerned.

It may be desirable to have in a warless world at least two new bodies for dealing with the substance of political disputes. In the first place, a world conciliation board could be empowered to investigate all disputes referred to it by one of the parties to a dispute. It should try to elucidate the facts and to bring the nations to an amicable settlement. Very often, once all facts are known and objectively presented, the passions may subside and the parties may be willing to listen to suggestions from the conciliation board for the adjustment of their dispute.

If this method does not result in a settlement, or if the parties are not willing to resort to it, another approach may be tried. It will involve a political decision by the General Assembly at the beginning and the end of the process, but the central decision on the merits of the dispute may be referred to an impartial body. At the beginning, the General Assembly will have to determine that a particular dispute cannot be effectively settled by reference to the International Court of Justice, that it is likely to endanger peace, and that it must be settled before it reaches the explosive stage. Then the Assembly will refer the matter to a world arbitral tribunal, composed of some fifteen or seventeen persons, preferably elder statesmen well known to all, whose experience and reputation will furnish the best assurance of impartiality and breadth of view. The tribunal will consider all aspects of the dispute and will prepare recommendations for a comprehensive solution, based on what it deems to be reasonable, just, and fair to all concerned. For instance, if there should be a boundary dispute in which one side clearly has the legal title to the territory but the other side claims it on the basis of the wishes of its inhabitants, the tribunal may not only order a plebiscite to ascertain the views of the local population, but may also order the second state to compensate the first one for the lost territory by special economic concessions or by other means which will permit the loser to accept the decision without a loss of face.

It may be expected that the recommendations of the tribunal will have such great moral weight that the parties will not dare to reject them. But if any nation shall reject them, the matter will be referred back to the General Assembly, which may deem the situation so dangerous and the solution proposed by the tribunal so satisfactory that it may be willing to impose it upon the recalcitrant party or parties. To ensure a proper backing for such a decision, a preponderant majority in the Assembly may be required (e.g., a three-fourths majority including two thirds of the twelve major powers). Once adopted, such a decision may be enforced through economic sanctions or even by a limited use of the international peace force. Pressure for voluntary acceptance is likely to be so strong, however, that resort to forcible means of execution will seldom be required.

In this manner, in a disarmed world nations can be protected by the international peace force against aggression by another nation, while at the same time means can be provided for peaceful change of intolerable situations which could easily lead to a disturbance of peace. A strengthened United Nations will carefully supervise these new activities in order to ensure that they are not abused. A code of world law will also be established which will impose limits not only on certain activities of states, such as aggression, direct and indirect, and subversion, but will also prescribe the circumstances in which the international peace force will be entitled to take action. A further check may be provided through the International Court of Justice which may be empowered to declare certain acts of the force, of the arbitral tribunal, or of the United Nations itself, illegal because of their inconsistency with such a code. Thus the danger of tyranny in a peaceful world will be reduced, and the rule of law and justice will be ensured. The task is tremendous, the obstacles are great, but as President Kennedy has said: "Never have the nations of the world had so much to lose—or so much to gain. Together we shall save our planet, or together we shall perish in its flames. . . . We must create even as we destroy—creating worldwide law and law enforcement as we outlaw worldwide war and weapons."

# II

## Increasing security through disarmament

BY JULES MOCH

Former member of French delegation
to the General Assembly
and former Permanent Representative
of France on the United Nations
Disarmament Commission

"Let us suppose the problem solved," to use a favorite phrase of
the mathematician. The world is disarmed. It is now a question
of demonstrating that the security of the various peoples is better
assured than when their landscape bristled with launching pads,
with batteries, and with arsenals, and when their young people
uselessly spent the best years of their lives in barracks and training camps.

Our demonstration supposes the realization of four conditions:

(1) The International Control Organization for Disarmament
has reached full achievement of disarmament and possesses the
most extensive powers of inspection in order to expose any attempt at clandestine rearmament.

(2) The International Court of Justice lays down the law.
Contrary to the present situation, its jurisdiction is compulsory
on the suit of a single party. Its judgments have effective force
in all countries in the same way as the internal laws of those
countries. It can punish states in the same manner as the courts
ruling in criminal or civil matters, not of course by deprivation
of liberty—one cannot imprison an entire nation—but by fines,
injunctions, and penalties. It can also impose economic sanctions.

(3) Where the foregoing measures are inadequate, the Court
is so established—the treaty will have set up this procedure—as

to put in motion either directly, or indirectly through a peace-keeping machinery or the Security Council, an International Police Force which will intervene by blockade or by occupation of the territory which has revolted against international law. If this action is to be decided by the Security Council, the Charter will previously have been modified in order to abolish the veto which would block application of the Court's judgments, since this veto, a vestige of the absolute sovereignty of five states, is incompatible with the supremacy of international law.

(4) The International Police Force will have been created before the completion of disarmament. For our purposes it matters little whether the police force is composed of men individually recruited by the International Organization and permanently in its service or of contingents of national police temporarily placed at its disposal. The first solution is more rational and more reliable, the second less costly and more in line with the traditions of states not yet accustomed to the loss of their total sovereignty in an area which they have always felt to be most vital. Whether a permanent and autonomous force or a temporary amalgamation of national contingents, the police force has at its disposal a complement superior to that of the largest national army, as well as means of rapid transportation.

Having given a hypothetical reality to the preceding system, let us try to measure the risks which disarmed states will incur. They are technical, political, and social. The first involve the launching of an aggressive attack, and are the result of the concealment of materials, possibly during the course of disarmament, or of clandestine manufacture begun after the completion of disarmament. The second are those springing from bellicose propaganda or from subversive activities. The last are the consequences of the elimination of military service and the conversion of war industries.

Before examining them, let us make a general observation: the distrust of disarmament is just as great as the hope placed in it. How many times have we heard people who believe themselves well informed say: "If you take from men their most murderous weapons, they will fight with rifles and revolvers. If you take away their last pistol, they will attack each other with clubs and fists. You will never change human nature."

We must have a more hopeful view. The more civilized men become, the more they raise their standard of living and the less they value military glory. Primitive man is bellicose because his ancestors, in order to ensure their survival, had to triumph over other men. But in the twentieth century, in spite of the monstrous exceptions of some dictators, the joy, purity, and nobility of war belong to the past. The GIs and Tommies were not overcome with joy when they disembarked in France to help the poilus chase away the "Fritz." The they-must-be-crushed attitude expressed more a necessity than enthusiasm. The "taste for war" is dead.

What is true of the peoples of the West is also true of the Soviets, who are just as profoundly devoted to peace. The evolution of China toward less poverty will produce the same result in Asia. Let us put aside therefore the supposition which imagines millions of Russians, and yellow and black peoples, brandishing spears, scythes, or crossbows as they rush to attack the prosperous and disarmed nations. Let us confine ourselves to the possibilities of sabotage of disarmament or of clandestine rearmament. Are these conceivable?

In replying objectively to such a question, let us not forget our initial assumptions: there is an International Control Organization; the Court of Justice is functioning; and the International Police Force has been established.

Let us look first at the risk of cheating in the course of disarmament.

In regard to conventional arms, the experience of the Second World War teaches us that small quantities of war material, even large items, can be hidden, with the complicity of military authorities, during the carrying out of disarmament. The members of the French Resistance hid tanks under straw in barns, and the German authorities never found them. A few small private planes, disassembled, were similarly hidden, and were put together at the time of the Liberation. Further, depots of light arms —machine guns, recoilless artillery, and explosive charges—were established, thanks in part to parachute drops, making it possible to arm the underground.

But all this was not a large operation by our terms and it certainly took place in a context very different from ours. Control was at that time the business of the occupying power, the temporarily victorious enemy. It was a patriotic duty to neutralize this. Those who hid arms always had the moral support and often the actual assistance of the population.

By contrast, control of the disarmed world will be carried out in peace, and internationally with ample participation on the part of the state being inspected. A state's representatives would be obliged to play an almost inconceivably difficult double game if they tried to circumvent control while collaborating with it.

Moreover, public opinion, which was favorable to the underground movements of World War II, would be hostile to any disturbers of the peace who might try to maintain a clandestine military potential in a disarmed state.

The risk of arms concealment, then, is virtually negligible.

There remains in the area of conventional weapons the other aspect of risk: clandestine rearmament after the destruction of armaments.

The control organization will certainly never be able to inspect on a permanent basis all the factories of a country, and as a possibility, we must concede that armaments could be produced in secret. An ingot of steel can become just as easily the barrel of a cannon as the axle of a locomotive, and the same lathe can sometimes machine the one and the other. A French gear factory in 1914, after the battle of the Marne, improvised a chain process of machine-finishing for shell casings and became quickly the principal producer before reconverting in 1918 to an automobile factory.

This versatility can be carried even further: some industries having no conceivable connection with military manufacture can at times be converted to arms production. The failure to exploit to the full the victory of the Marne in September, 1914, was due not only to the fatigue of our soldiers but also, and especially, to the lack of 75-millimeter shells, consumption having exceeded all expectations of the strategists. One battery near the position I was occupying at that time received shells made of glass which had been furnished to the gunpowder factory by a manufacturer of bottles! The artillery men, fearing explosion in the bores of the guns, took cover before firing. In fact, the shells burst on target, making just as much noise and smoke, and probably doing as much damage, as steel or steel-coated cast-iron projectiles. Does it follow, now, that the disarmament control organization should maintain constant surveillance in glass factories?

Obviously not! Here again the situation in a disarmed world differs completely from that in a country at war. One cannot imagine glassmakers being unaware of the substitution of shells for bottles in their production lines, or of making themselves accomplices in this sabotage of peace. However, granting that armaments could be secretly manufactured on a small scale, it would certainly not be possible to undertake the large-scale assembly-line production which is necessary for an aggression.

For we must not forget that in our hypothesis it is not only the loyally disarmed neighbor that a traitorous state would attack: an attack would have to be made against the whole civilized world; and the criminal state would incur the world's moral condemnation, about which it might not perhaps care very much, but in addition it would be obliged to suffer economic sanctions which in the world as it would then be organized would be immediate. Finally, if these measures did not halt the offensive, the International Police Force would intervene, drawing arms from the stocks of the International Organization accumulated for that purpose.

This would be then a truly conventional war which would be waged in the defense of law under the auspices of the International Organization, and the aggressor would not have been able to arm himself clandestinely to the degree necessary to enable him to defeat a coalition of the whole world.

Let us also not be deeply concerned about the often mentioned —and exaggerated—danger of the transformation of peacetime vehicles into instruments of war.

It is easy to assert that the aggressor state would be able to convert its commercial planes into bombers and its merchant vessels into cruisers. It is less easy to bring about these metamorphoses effectively.

In our hypothetical world, the fleets of military aircraft which are today numbered in thousands of airplanes for each of the great military powers, will have been consigned to the scrap heap, or converted for other uses. The states will have at their disposal only their commercial and private airplanes, which in each country represent only a few hundred medium or long-range planes.

A transport plane of recent model can, to be sure, be converted into a bomber in the sense that one can fasten to its fuselage a few bombs manufactured secretly. This will not change it into a valuable piece of war equipment: the plane will still lack all the special apparatus, particularly the bombsight and all the rapid-fire defensive armament, delicate equipment which could not be improvised, and could not be manufactured without the knowledge of the control organization. Badly adapted to its war mission and a mediocre combat unit, it will be an easy prey for the fighter planes of the international police.

Similarly, it is not enough to install a small caliber gun on the deck of a cargo ship, a banana boat, or an oil tanker, if one wishes to possess a cruiser. It is in this manner that merchant ships were armed during the last war. At the very most, we thus enabled them to defend themselves against a surface attack by a submarine. Such armed craft possessed none of the characteristics of a combat vessel: speed, aiming devices, fire-control center, antiaircraft and antisubmarine defense, and so on.

In either of these cases, moreover, how can one count on the silent complicity of the workers carrying out this "militarization," and of the sailors or of the civil aviators who become aware of it? Here again the deception and the danger would be quickly publicized, even if only anonymously, to the international inspectors.

Thus, always in terms of our basic hypotheses, the security of the disarmed and loyal nations appears virtually complete so far as conventional armaments are concerned.

In the nuclear realm, we must examine successively the resumption of production of fissionable materials for military purposes, recourse to pre-existing stocks that have been hidden, and the problem of delivery vehicles.

First of all, it is impossible to conceive of a clandestine resumption of production of fissionable materials. To prevent it, we have only to place permanent inspectors in two types of factories which, because of their dimensions and complexity, cannot be camouflaged. Those separating fissionable uranium from natural uranium, of which it constitutes only seven thousandths of a part, extend over immense areas and operate in long chains. One has only to curtail the final stages of this production to limit the percentage of enrichment to a degree permitting all peaceful applications, but prohibiting the purity necessary for explosion. It is obviously impossible to re-establish secretly those stages of the chain that have been removed.

The other plants, those recovering the materials created in the transformation of the bars used by the reactors, must continue their operation; they must be given complete freedom, not only to regenerate the bars but also to extract from them the radio-isotopes, many of which already have peaceful applications while others will reveal their uses as knowledge of them increases. Among these elements is plutonium, the second primary material of bombs, the extraction of which can scarcely be halted, but must be controlled. This dangerous metal, which kills a man who is exposed to the tiniest fragment of its dust, has no practical use except for the bomb, and, very fortunately, cannot exist in nature. There will be good reason, then, if extraction cannot be prohibited, to keep careful account of the results, and to control subsequent transfers of the metal, whether to industries which would have found a means of using it peacefully and without risk, or to storage areas. The extraction and handling process behind protective concrete walls is so delicate that no clandestine operation need be feared.

These two groups of factories are not numerous: several dozen in all on the surface of the earth. Some years ago it was calculated that a group of about three thousand inspectors—one-third of them engineers and two-thirds technicians—would be sufficient to give to the world the assurance that no more secret manufacture of fissionable material for military purposes exists on the earth.

There now remains the question of stockpiles of nuclear bombs, of nuclear warheads for rockets and satellites, and of fissionable material for military purposes, all established prior to the creation of the International Control Organization.

The treaty has, according to our hypothesis, provided for an entire series of reconversions: scrapping all metallic things, denaturing fissionable uranium by adding its inert isotope, transforming thorium, storing plutonium, and so on. But will the peoples of the world have assurance that all these agreements have been strictly carried out?

No one today, alas, can any longer give this assurance. More than ten years ago, I pointed out to the United Nations that humanity had passed the point which transatlantic aviators of the heroic age called "the point of no return." For the "disarmers" of today the point of no return was the point before which an effective control of past production was still possible, and beyond which such control becomes illusory.

An example will clarify this statement. Knowing the producing plants (their size prevents their being hidden), the date of their construction, their maximum electric-power absorption, and their manufacturing processes, engineers can evaluate their past production within 20 to 25 per cent. If computations give for a new plant a production of 50 kg., the margin of error—10 to 12 kg.—would be hardly enough for the "critical mass" constituting the lower limit for arming a bomb. At this point, it is simple to require the plant director to account for the use of this material: the amount that he might attempt to hide would not be enough to arm a bomb. The control is, therefore, effective.

But if the past production amounts to several hundred tons— as is today the case in the United States and in Soviet Russia —the same 20 per cent margin of uncertainty would represent a possible concealment of several dozens of tons, and, therefore, of several thousand bombs. When one considers that only twenty of these bombs are needed to lay waste a country the size of France, the control no longer provides, then, any real security. We have reached that point!

For this reason, the principal effort of the permanent control organization must be concentrated not on the bomb, but on the separate parts of the bomb's machinery, and on the means of delivery to the target.

The different navigational parts of the long-range rocket or of the satellite—gyroscopes, electronic and radio-electronic instruments—are not only "miniaturized" but involve also a very high precision in their manufacture. These are difficult conditions to meet, and reduce to a very small number the highly specialized plants capable of producing the parts. Consequently, an almost permanent but relatively easy check on the secret manufacture of this equipment and of its repair or mounting on existing rockets would be necessary.

However, it is the control of the delivery vehicles which will give the greatest security, if it is established in time. The first generation of long-range rockets reached a per-unit weight of about 100 tons, and the second, about 40 tons. Their launching pads, veritable steel cathedrals, cannot be camouflaged or built secretly. The ships and airplanes capable of launching these missiles are huge and depend on naval dockyards or airfields of the sort that are few in number, furnished abundantly with special equipment and easy to find. If the control had been established during the period of use of these two generations of missiles, it would have been completely effective in the disarmed world of our hypothesis.

But if the agreement for peace is further delayed, the rockets of the third generation will in turn have become operational, on one side as well as the other. Of similar power and range, they will weigh no more than about 10 tons, and will be launched from a submerged submarine or from a freight car supported by hydraulic jacks, or from a pit covered until the moment of firing.

The threat thus grows worse from month to month: a new "point of no return" looms on the horizon. The general public is too little aware of the fact that a single atomic submarine, whose period of submersion is limited only by the strength of its crew's nerves, armed with sixteen missiles similar to the type of the American *Polaris* or to its Soviet counterpart, possesses *a fire-power and a destructive capacity several times greater than the total expended by all the land, sea, and air forces on both sides all through the ten years of the two world wars!* Worse still: it is practically impossible to find this diabolical vessel, and, if it submerges at a point in the vast seas properly chosen, it can, even with the present 1,500-mile range of its missiles, devastate any area of the globe, no point of which is in fact located more than 1,500 miles from an ocean. The increase now being sought in the range of these missiles—the talk is of of 2,000 miles, even 4,000—is not an attempt to strike, should the occasion arise, at new parts of the earth, but is simply a question of reducing the distance to be covered under water by the submarine before it launches its apocalyptic fire.

Is there, then, no hope for the security of the disarmed world? I believe that there is: the atomic submarines cannot be hidden, at least when they return to the base to recharge their reactors, even though this may occur only once a year. Neither can they be built secretly. Their bases, moreover, will have been reconverted during the carrying out of the treaty. How could a *Nautilus* continue to wander under the surface of the seas without supplies or repairs?

There remains the problem of the 10-ton missiles launched from underground silos, or even from underwater towers hidden in permanent locations. The risk remains that some of these may have been clandestinely retained. But there is no fear of new ones being constructed: the processes are too intricate to be undertaken anywhere except in large and highly specialized plants which would, therefore, be well known and controlled. What we have said about miniaturized equipment applies also to the missiles that have been reduced in size.

Does the possible existence of limited stocks of third generation rockets—and also of chemical or biological weapons of mass destruction, which are even easier to hide—force the world to give up all hope of security through disarmament? No, not at all. For it is one thing to hide stocks of weapons at the time when the treaty enters into force and is put into effect, when, facing the risks of a leap into the unknown, patriotism can be put forward as an excuse. It is quite another matter to conserve these stocks after the treaty has been faithfully carried out by all the states, and in so doing to become liable to international sanctions while being outlawed by humanity.

It is just possible to imagine that military staffs, attached to their traditions and on the point of being dissolved, would suppose it a duty to build up secret stocks before being disbanded although such a supposition might appear rash to others. It is difficult to imagine, however, that the rulers of this same state will, after a few years of regular operation of the treaty, wish to retain such stocks and keep them ready for use. The material damage resulting from the discovery of such hidden stocks by an inspection set on foot, for example, by an anonymous accusation, would be too great.

At this point we leave the realm of the technical to consider the moral, psychological, and political aspects of security.

Disarmament will work deep changes in the behavior of citizens. Their grandparents lived in constant fear of unemployment, accidents, illness, invalidism, and old age, any one of which would deprive their family of bread. The development of social legislation, in varying degree—to be sure—according to the different kinds of government, but an evolution seen throughout the world, has dispelled such fears. It has created a new kind of wage earner, confident of tomorrow, less inclined to saving, getting more out of life, traveling (thanks to paid holidays), discovering horizons other than those of the workshop and the home, acquiring a liking for a new comfort which is more and more within reach, and buying household appliances, even an automobile, on the installment plan.

Even in countries such as France where social progress is well advanced, our contemporaries are passing through only the first part of their own transformation. Although recent, the change is profound. The young Frenchmen of today cannot imagine a job which would not include paid holidays, collective bargaining, and elected committees managing the workers' social advancement. They are astounded when one points out to them that in France the first of these reforms is only twenty-six years old, and that before the government of Léon Blum in 1936, their fathers worked every day of the year, except Sundays and national holidays.

If men have been changed in this manner as individuals, they will undergo changes no less profound when war will have been made impossible. Europeans are still steeped in memories of invasions, air raids, ruins, massacres, executions of prisoners, and genocide. They can still see the long lines of civilian refugees, who had lost everything, and were machine-gunned from the air as they fled along the roads. Europeans do not want to see that again, and they are ready to pay any price to avoid it. But at the same time, their distrust is above reproach as long as war remains a possibility. For these horrible memories are long-lived. At the beginning of the twentieth century, the Rhinelanders still recounted stories of the burning of the Palatinate by the French in 1688—stories expanded by the telling through half a dozen generations. The misdeeds of the Prussian Uhlans of 1870 horrified me when I heard about them thirty years later. The gas chambers of Hitler remain an abomination, and we tend to hold his countrymen collectively responsible for them.

Knowing that since the beginning of this so-called civilized century peace has not reigned throughout the world for more than five or six years at a time, and that men have been killing each other constantly in one continent or another, how can men and women avoid being anxious, distrustful, and even xenophobic? Why should they not agree to assure their defense against neighbors whom they suspect and to whom they ascribe the most hostile designs? Why should they not vote, on both sides of the frontier, for the armament race which is presented to them as a guarantee of peace, while in fact it increases the risks of war? All the drama of the continued existence of humanity is found in this almost universal state of mind.

Here, as in so many other areas, common sense is making headway. If the French, for example, are not forgetting the crimes of Hitler which plunged so many families into mourning, they are learning little by little that they cannot blame the new generation of Germans, at least those who were too young to be Nazis. In spite of the fact that too many Nazis have kept their posts in the two German states, we have sketched out the necessary reconciliation between two peoples condemned by geography to live side by side, while set by history, down through the centuries, one against the other.

Progress is even more rapid in parts of Western Europe than it is between the Americans and the Russians, who constantly see in each other's actions the worst intentions, although they have never been enemies. The Russians seem to have forgotten the masses of supplies they received during the war; the Americans the bloody epic of Stalingrad which made possible the long preparation for the Liberation landings.

After these general remarks, let us return to our basic hypothesis: the treaty is properly carried out and controlled. Very quickly the feeling of insecurity gives way to an immense relief. Instinctive at the start—one distrusts good fortune—it soon becomes rational and profound. The international atmosphere becomes relaxed with a return to calm in diplomacy, the remaining political disputes are settled or appear insignificant—and how insignificant!—compared to what was at stake in the treaty. How is it possible, for example, to wrangle over Berlin when peace is established and the progressive disappearance of armies will make it necessary to turn this city into one of the first garrisons of the international police? After the agreement between East and West, both the fearful political games and the Asiatic shrewdness will disappear. Even the Chinese problem will of necessity have been resolved because the treaty could not come into effect without the countersignature of China, which possesses the largest army and which will have undoubtedly become, while the disarmament negotiations are in progress, the fifth atomic power. This signature will, by a no less impelling necessity, have been preceded or accompanied by the substitution, too long delayed, of the China of Peking for that of Formosa in the world organizations.

Advancement toward the disarmed security of nations and progress toward the moral disarmament of men will go hand in hand: irreversible forces, each one will accelerate and promote the other.

We must have in this a confidence which although absolute is none the less rational. How could the evolution be otherwise? Already, in our uncertain, suspicious, overarmed world, disarmament is the aspiration of the people, more even than of the governments whose responsibilities lead them to surround themselves with outmoded safeguards. With the exception of a few senseless agitators, millions—even billions—of men when asked, "Do you want a stable and lasting peace?" would answer without hesitation "Yes" and become indignant at the thought that one could ask such a question.

The American worker's desire for peace is no greater than that of his Soviet comrade, even though, unlike the latter, he is not lulled and nagged at work, at his club, at his union office, at his rest camp, and even in the streets by the slogan *Mirou Mir!*—Peace in the World!

This collective evolution toward the certainty of national security, just as the evolution of the individual moves him toward social security, will make men vigilant guardians of the advantages thus acquired or won. If rulers, traitors to the cause of peace, should try to prepare a secret aggression, they would encounter, probably even in a totalitarian state, passive resistance and anonymous denunciations which would eventually reach the ears of the International Control Organization, a safeguard not to be underestimated.

Another hypothesis: a possible aggressor wishes to condition public opinion, to win it over to a policy of war by pretending that security is threatened—in other words, the usual type of propaganda of the armament-race era in all the countries. There is, however, a major difference between yesterday and tomorrow: the International Control Organization, immediately advised of this campaign, which could not be clandestine, will make a judgment concerning the reality of the motives set forth and will move this two-nation dispute onto the international level in order to bring about an impartial study of it and a peaceful settlement.

Thus, wherever one looks, unarmed peace contains in itself and brings to the hearts of men the power that makes it unconquerable.

Two other factors modify in the same direction the behavior of man: the new spirit in teaching and the disappearance of military barracks.

In a disarmed world, the education of the young will be profoundly changed, perhaps even in spite of the curriculum and unbeknown to the teachers, for the scale of values will no longer be the same. Consider in this regard especially the study of national history and civic virtues. History as it has always been taught is an unending tale of coalitions, campaigns, and treaties, laying greater stress on the victories which are, of course, glorious, than on the defeats, which are always accidental. Austerlitz is of much greater importance in France than is Trafalgar, which is invariably presented as a monumental example of duplicity; the expression "a Trafalgar trick," still used at the end of the last century, is synonomous with "a shabby maneuver."

The spirit of the teaching of history changed, in France at least, at the beginning of the century, when I was young. My family admired the new textbooks, in which emphasis was put more on the evolution of civilizations than on the feats of arms of the rulers. However, these deeds were still taught, and with too many details. In the schools of my childhood, the tearing away from the mother country of Alsace and Lorraine, imposed upon these provinces by the government, and the incidents which arose between French patriots of these regions and German soldiers garrisoned there, had profound repercussions on the teachings of the schoolmasters and on the minds of the pupils. At that time two schoolboys out of three studied German in preference to all other foreign languages, not because it would be more useful in their lives, but because their parents, even though members of the generation following the Franco-Prussian War, still held the conviction—unexpressed but present beneath the surface—that the war for liberation of the two provinces would come sooner or later and that their sons, as soldiers, must know the language of the enemy. An absurd idea, but one which had an influence on the formation of our minds. I mention this in order to emphasize the extent to which the fear and the expectation of conflict can weigh upon teaching and can prepare whole generations of young people who, although not loving war, do not stand up with all their strength against war because they accept the possibility or inevitability of it.

Let us imagine now the results of a quarter century of teaching in a disarmed world. The men who are shaped by this will have undoubtedly a greater horror of war than those who have waged it, whom they will consider at fault, not only because they were not able to avoid it, but also because they accepted the consequences.

I am not a conscientious objector, even though as France's Minister of Defense I set free those who were. I fought "honorably" from beginning to end all through the ten years of the two world wars, the second time as a volunteer. A fifth part of my life has thus been given over to battle, in uniform and in the Resistance. I am convinced, however, that in the period the characteristics of which we are trying to analyze, those who will be considered the truly "civilized" men of the first half of our century will not be the generals, officers, and soldiers of the two wars but rather the conscientious objectors, the proponents of neutrality, the men who, like Romain Rolland, wished to remain "above the mêlée," according to the title of the book (*Au dessus de la mêlée*) which he published in Switzerland in 1915 and which became—justifiably at that time—a scandal in France.

Let me say again that, when I was defending my country and its liberty in the trenches and on the sea, I did not approve of this form of resistance to war. But I am certain that the young of the disarmed era will glorify these forerunners—a probable evolution which will, in turn, strengthen the stability of peace.

Another change favorable to the behavior of future generations would be the elimination of the compulsory year or more of military training and barracks life at the time when temperaments are becoming distinct and vocational decisions are emerging. My experience with obligatory military service in 1912 taught me that the army in peacetime is not a school which teaches the virtue of nobility and devotion to the public good. In the promiscuity of the barracks and that of the nearby tavern, the recruits learn above all to avoid work, "to goldbrick," as it is expressed nowadays. The most delinquent recruits corrupt the well-bred. The moral line of march is down rather than up.

In addition, the young soldier comes under the influence of instructors, career soldiers, many of whom do not have a vocation as educators. The discipline is naturally directed toward the exigencies of war. To prepare for war is to become accustomed to the idea that war may occur, and this deforms the spirit. Chauvinism then wreaks its ravages. The "psychology" of the army is above all the teaching of brutality, even xenophobia.

In the disarmed world, the ill deeds of military training will be erased, while the considerable benefits of its physical-training programs will be carried on under civilian auspices.

We must turn, now, to another and more delicate aspect of

security in a disarmed world: the risk of subversive action. It is important first to define this expression, often generalized and distorted.

Perhaps I shall shock some readers by restricting the term sharply. Being a democrat, in the European sense of the word, I profess that all opinions, without exception, have the right to be expressed freely. In my opinion, there is no true democracy in any place where the law prohibits any thought from being made known.

Let me speak even more plainly. I am not a Communist. I gave proof of this, as some readers will perhaps remember, when, as France's Minister of the Interior from 1947 to 1950, I defended the regime by opposing the political strikes set in motion by the Communists in 1947 and in 1948. It was the time of the break between the U. S. S. R. and the West, which brought about the departure of the Communists from the governments in which they had participated in Belgium, in Italy, and elsewhere, or their exclusion from power, as in France. The stakes were the same in France as were gambled and lost, among waves of strikes, in Czechoslovakia. In order to keep Paris from suffering the fate of Prague, I went through some difficult hours. But even then I never dreamed of asking that the Communist Party—which I was fighting fiercely—be outlawed, and I should have opposed such a proposition if any Deputy had initiated it.

The division between what is legal and what is prohibited lies, in my opinion, on the boundary between propaganda and conspiracy.

In a democracy all propaganda must be permitted. A party has the right to announce that its victory at the polls would mean the end of fundamental liberties and the beginning of the dictatorship of a single party, clan, group, caste, or even one man. It is up to the voters to have the good sense to block this party by their votes.

Thus, a Communist regime, brought to power by the majority of the electorate normally and freely consulted, is as legitimate as any other political regime that wins the elections—although so much the worse for the voters who choose this path!

What should be suppressed, on the other hand, is the revolutionary action of active minorities preparing secretly to take over the power by force or by guile and without the consent of the voters. This is the only meaning a French democrat can give to the expression "subversive action."

On this basis, external help given to propaganda carried on within the law of a government—even that which tries to replace the government by constitutional means—is legal, whether it comes from Moscow, from Rome, or from foreign economic groups.

If foreign support is limited to gifts of money, often hidden in price increases on regular transactions or in agents' commissions, to subsidies for newspapers operating at a loss, to political or quasi-political organizations, to radio appeals, to supplies of tracts or books sold beneath their cost price—all cases that I came across during the 1947–48 period—it is difficult to see how it can be prohibited within the context of democratic principles. It must be countered by being exposed to public opinion. This is a good way, at least in France—as I have been able to demonstrate.

We blame the Soviets for such actions. Are we innocent of the same charge? Is not anti-Communist propaganda carried on just as continuously, if not as skillfully, and with external aid? Let us not press the point but simply express the hope, without too much faith, that in a world at peace such campaigns will cease, or, at least, will lose their influence, if indeed they have ever had any influence of importance on either side.

There remains the possibility of true subversive action: the supplying of weapons and volunteers by foreigners to a clandestine movement sharing their ideology. This is a risk that cannot be excluded from our completely disarmed world. Even in small amounts, the hidden shipments could become dangerous, for national police forces would have reduced complements at their disposal. In the disarmament negotiations it has been proposed that there be one policeman for every five hundred or thousand inhabitants, which in France would amount to 46,000 to 92,000 men. An underground movement can possess secret commandos which, although not equal in numbers, would profit by the advantage of surprise and by a concentrated attack on the nerve centers, with the police scattered all over the territory. If they received equipment from the outside equal to that of the police, they could try their luck. What counteraction would be feasible?

There is, first of all, one possibility which must be ruled out: the threatened country making an appeal *against its own citizens* to the International Control Organization responsible for the maintenance of the peace. This is an inadmissible solution even if the government proves that it legitimately represents its country. First, such proof is difficult to establish; almost all governments have begun by being "revolutionary." At what point have they ceased to be revolutionary by acquiring that quality which authorizes the world to intervene on their behalf? One can imagine the degree of controversy on such a subject. Secondly, if it followed this line of action, the International Organization would be changed into a modern Holy Alliance, dedicated to the defense of existing regimes. In the beginning it would act for the interested peoples, but undoubtedly it would soon turn against them.

Let us establish in principle, then, that the internal affairs of a country, such as the conflicts between a government and a group of its citizens or between two groups of citizens, concern only that country, even in a disarmed world. On the other hand, international parrying action against subversive activities is legal when the government concerned can prove that a foreign intervention has occurred in the form of shipments of arms or in the presence of foreign volunteers.

One of the important clauses of the treaty for general and complete disarmament will in fact be the prohibition of all arms shipments, whether these come from authorized stockpiles of the national police or from hidden depots, or departures of volunteers, whether dispatched by a foreign government or by groups of its citizens for whose actions it is responsible. If, therefore, the threatened regime can provide proof that such acts have taken place, it is *ipso facto* in a state of legitimate defense and has a right to international assistance, not against its own nationals but against the state supporting them. In this context, the foreign subversive action must, according to the terms of the treaty, be likened to an aggression, on condition, of course, that this conclusion will not apply to the many forms of propaganda.

The final aspect of the problem, the economic and social risks involved in disarmament, I mention only to make my discussion complete.

A consultative group of the United Nations, comprising representatives of ten powers, including the four atomic powers, studied this question in 1962. It arrived at the unanimous conclusion—Russians and Americans in agreement this time—that given certain precautions these risks are nonexistent. There are so many possibilities for using the resources made available by the elimination throughout the whole world of annual military expenditures of *one hundred and twenty billions of dollars— 3,800 dollars per second!*—that the real problem will be *to establish priorities* among the substitute needs to be fulfilled: individual consumption in the underdeveloped countries, increase in production capacity, social investments, etc.

The experts emphasize that reconversion at the end of the Second World War "was a much larger one and involved a more rapid transfer of resources than total disarmament would require at present," that the massive demobilizations at that time did not increase unemployment appreciably, and that "the pace of recovery, particularly of industrial output, was impressively rapid." It would be necessary, obviously, to have prepared such a reconversion in advance to avoid some local problems—especially in the wartime ports. Some precautions, some adaptations, some new specializations will certainly be necessary; but the total demand for products will be maintained, in spite of the elimination of military purchases, both in capitalistic states and in those with dictatorial planning.

Without entering into detail, we can all agree that total disarmament involves, within the given hypotheses, no serious risk to states applying it faithfully and that it will give a greater priority to social undertakings, a general improvement in standards of living, better prospects for the young entering adult life, for whom there would no longer be any separation from the family for compulsory military service, and a reduction of the tension among nations and races.

*A long life, then, to general and complete disarmament, internationally controlled, the supreme hope of mankind!*

# III

## Change in a disarmed world

BY ARNOLD TOYNBEE

Historian, The Royal Institute
of International Affairs, London

It is being assumed in this book that human force and power—spiritual, of course, as well as physical—have been reordered in a way that has effectively deprived the world's local states of their traditional liberty to go to war. In other words, sovereignty has been transferred, in effect, from the local states to a world state. At least the minimum amount of power and authority that is required for the effective maintenance of world peace has been centralized, so it is being assumed, in the hands of what, in virtue of this, can properly be called a world government, though it may still be a rudimentary one for other purposes.

In many Western minds the first reaction to these assumptions is likely perhaps to be negative. The assumptions may strike a Westerner as being so utopian that speculations founded on them will be hardly worth making. They stand condemned in advance. In Western history hitherto, the occasional attempts to impose peace through unity have, in fact, all been abortive. Hitler, Napoleon, Charles V, Otto I, Charlemagne: each in turn has been worsted. To find these assumptions translated into Western realities, we have to go back more than fifteen hundred years. Peace through unity was a reality in the Western provinces of the Roman Empire before the Empire's decline and fall in this fringe of its domain. But, for Westerners, their Roman past has, long since, become "ancient history." It has become, for us, something so remote that we do not even feel any nostalgia for it—greatly though we yearn for unity and peace in our time.

Fortunately, however, for the future of the human race, we Westerners are a minority and our sad experience in public affairs has been an exceptional one. In the historical experience of the greater part of mankind, the state of affairs that is being assumed in this book has been a comparatively recent reality. In China, India, and Pakistan, there has been a world state within living memory. The world state in China that finally foundered in 1911 had by then been in existence, off and on, for more than twenty-one centuries. The world state in the Indian subcontinent that split in 1947 had been in existence for one century and had had several predecessors. The world state in Japan that was reduced to being a local state in 1868 had been maintaining itself as a world state for more than two centuries before that.

But how can there ever have been a world state in one group of not very large islands adjoining the largest of the continents? And how can even subcontinents, such as China and India are, be equivalents of the whole wide world? The answer is that thinking makes them so. The smallest human community constitutes the whole world for the people inside it if it is insulated from all other human communities on the face of the planet; and it will be insulated from them if its members feel that outsiders do not count. In this sense—and it is a very practical sense—even tiny Japan was a world state during her two centuries of insulation under the regime of the Tokugawa Shoguns. In the same sense the Chinese Empire and the Roman Empire were world states *a fortiori*. In the eyes of its citizens, each of these two empires embraced the entire civilized world. The tribes outside the pale were insignificant barbarians.

It is worth seeing what light the histories of these virtual world states can throw on the question of internal change and revolution in a warless world. For these worlds were all warless. The Roman Empire and the Chinese Empire were literally warless for several centuries on end; and, if and when they did fall into a bout of anarchy and disruption, they quickly recaptured their former state of unity and peace. It was only in the Roman Empire's backward Western provinces that the second breakdown of the Empire was never retrieved. In the Levant the Roman Empire lived on, first in a Byzantine Greek, and then in an Ottoman Turkish avatar, until the final dissolution of the Ottoman Roman Empire in the First World War.

At the present moment, we are conscious of the difficulty of transferring sovereignty from local states to a world authority. When once a local community has tasted sovereignty, it is apt to cling to it, whatever the cost of this to itself as well as to its neighbors. In the past, the transfer has occasionally been accomplished, as has been noted; but it has never been accomplished without extreme tribulation; this high cost of unity and peace has made them precious; consequently the world governments of the past have concentrated their energies on self-preservation; and they have tried to preserve themselves by a policy of freezing. They have tried to freeze not only their frontiers against the outer barbarians and not only the structure of public administration inside those frontiers. They have tried to freeze the private lives of their citizens as well.

The most notorious recent instance of this policy is that of the Tokugawa regime in Japan. After all foreigners had been banished on pain of death, except for one Dutch trading post marooned on the islet of Deshima, the Japanese were forbidden to possess sea-going ships and to read foreign books. The former war-making feudal principalities on which the Shogunate had imposed a compulsory peace were regimented in minute detail. The relations of the feudal lords with the central government and of the feudal lords' retainers with the feudal lords and of the peasants with the lords and with the retainers were laid down in precise regulations. The feudal lords were compelled to spend so many months of the year at the Shogun's court. Every Japanese family had to be registered as being affiliated with a Buddhist monastery, as evidence that it was not crypto-Christian. A Japanese philosopher's philosophy had to be Confucian of a particular school.

The Roman imperial government did not carry its internal regimentation to such lengths as this until after its first bout of anarchy. After that, it tried to salvage its tottering economy by compelling sons to take their fathers' professions and by chaining taxpayers to their municipal taxation districts. But there is a story which, whether true or *ben trovato,* indicates that the freezing of the economy was the Roman imperial government's aim even in the Empire's early days, when its economy was relatively prosperous.

One day, so this story goes, the emperor's secretary came into the emperor's study in a state of excitement. "Your Majesty," he said, "we have just had the news that a man has invented unbreakable glass. We thought that your Majesty would be interested to know of this, as you will no doubt wish to reward the man suitably for this valuable service to the community." Without looking up from the papers on his desk, the emperor muttered "Have that man put to death." The secretary, thinking he had misheard, repeated what he had said, and the emperor then repeated his orders. "But, your Majesty," the secretary exclaimed, "the poor man is a public benefactor, not a criminal," and at this point the overworked and overworried emperor lost his temper. "Do I really," he shouted, "have to justify my orders by explaining the obvious? Cannot you see for yourself that, if this man's invention is put on the market, it will throw the makers of ordinary glass out of work? The world's economic equilibrium will be upset, and then the world's political and military equilibrium will be in danger. Cannot you see that this man's vexatious invention threatens to undo all my predecessors' work, and all my work too? My predecessors established world unity and peace through blood and tears; I am preserving their achievements by hard labor. Have that man put to death, I tell you, and, more important still, make sure that the records of his invention are destroyed."

If there is any truth in this story, the emperor did succeed in postponing the marketing of unbreakable glass for about nineteen hundred years; but this achievement was not, of course, an important one. If unbreakable glass had been marketed in the first century of the Christian era, the Roman Empire's stability (such as it was) would not really have been menaced. This was the nightmare of a harassed ruler who was haunted by fears of a return of a recent state of anarchy that had been intolerable; and, like many harassed people, he missed a vital point in fussing over a trifle. Unbreakable glass was kept off the market for the next nineteen centuries; but the Roman Empire's economy was not kept going for longer than the next four centuries—not, that is to say, in the Western provinces.

There was a genuine economic menace there, of major proportions, which this emperor and his successors either did not perceive or else ignored because they despaired of being able to cope with it. This menace, which did materialize, and which was a principal cause of the Roman Empire's decline and fall in the West, was the increasing load that was being placed on a backward agricultural economy by the growth of economically parasitic cities. The Graeco-Roman civilization was an urban one, and, in the progressive Eastern provinces, the cities paid their way by being economically productive. They were hives of manufacturing industry and trade. In imitation of the East, the West, too, felt that it must build up cities for itself and must adorn them with expensive public buildings in the Eastern style; but these exotic cities in the West were an incubus on the countryside. Instead of being hives of industry, they were dens of *rentiers* who drew incomes from the surrounding agricultural lands without making any adequate economic or social return to the community.

This major economic miscarriage did have disastrous social and political consequences. In the Western provinces of the Empire, the third century of the Christian era saw peasant revolts, the fourth century saw the cities go bankrupt, the fifth century saw the countryside take its revenge on the cities and saw it bring the Empire itself to the ground in this part of its domain. The rural population sought to protect itself in the hands of big landlords; and power and wealth flowed into their hands out of the hands, not only of the urban *rentiers,* but of the central government as well. This was a countermovement to the transfer of power in the opposite direction—from local states to a world government—that had originally brought the Roman Empire into existence.

The internal history of Japan under the Tokugawa regime followed a similar course. The central government was so intent on keeping the feudal lords' wings clipped that it did not see, or not till too late, that in its efforts to keep this part of Japan's social system frozen, it was unintentionally setting other parts in motion. The central government deliberately made life expensive for the feudal lords during their compulsory annual residence in the capital. It was glad to see them financially embarrassed; it was not sorry to see them ruined outright. It was slow to wake up to the truth that, in diminishing the already limited power and wealth of the feudal lords, it was working, not for its own profit, but for the profit of a rising urban commercial and industrial middle class.

The romantic figures in the later years of the Tokugawa regime are the handful of intellectuals who met together, at the dead of night, to spell out Dutch manuals of Western science at the risk of their lives. They were defying the regime's ban on "dangerous thought," and they played their modest part in preparing the way for the revolution by which the regime was eventually to be overthrown. But the major role in the prelude to the Meiji Revolution was played, not by the intellectuals, and not in defiance of the law. It was played by the businessmen in broad daylight and with impunity. The Shoguns had not thought of forbidding the new urban business class to finance the feudal lords' compulsory overspending and so to get the lords into their debt and the lords' property into their pockets. While the Shoguns supposed that they were keeping the Japanese people's life frozen, a major economic revolution was taking place under their noses —and this a revolution that did not suit their policy. The Japanese Shogunate, like the Roman imperial government, was jealous of all potential competitors. It had no more intention of making the businessmen's fortunes than it had of letting the feudal lords retain theirs. It did not see that, in its efforts to keep its old competitors down, it was creating an opportunity for new competitors to rise.

The common experience of the virtual world states of the past does throw light on the domestic prospects of a literal world state, if we succeed in establishing one. The gist of the common experience is that it is impossible for a government to freeze human life, however hard it may try and however propitious the circumstances may seem to be. No government could have tried harder than the Tokugawa government in Japan during the period when it was keeping Japan insulated from the rest of the world. Yet the result was the total defeat of the Tokugawa Shogun's policy. They would have been defeated by the shift in the domestic balance of power, even if there had been no Western world, and no Western industrial revolution forging new weapons, to impinge on Japan from outside. In the Soviet Union under the present Communist regime, it looks as if comparable shifts in the domestic balance of power are taking place today, regardless of the efforts of an ostensibly omnipotent government to keep the country imprisoned in the strait jacket of the Communist system.

The historical evidence suggests that the policy of trying to freeze a domestic situation is foredoomed to failure—and this even if there is no intervention from outside. Human affairs will never freeze; they will always stew; and the sure effect of putting the lid on them is to make them boil over. We are assuming that war has been suppressed, and that revolution by force of arms has also been ruled out. The price of banning violence may be to slow down the pace of change, but it seems most improbable that the effect will be to bring change to a halt. The stream of human life will go on moving, even if only at glacier pace. Wealth and, with it, power will continue to pass from one class to another. Officially established ideologies will tacitly be put in cold storage while continuing nominally to be honored. Satellite states and subject races will gradually succeed in asserting their human rights. When the use of physical force as an instrument of social change is abandoned, the spiritual force, which Mahatma Gandhi released in India with such potent effect, will continue to do its transforming work. The Negro minority in the United States could never have asserted its human rights by force of arms, and the military victory of the North in the Civil War did not solve the problem either. In so far as it is being solved in our time, it is being solved by the force of conscience. The fifth column that is sapping the Southern whites' resistance to the doing of social justice is an awareness in their own hearts that their cause is not, after all, a just one.

Attempts to freeze a situation are apt to have the opposite

effect to what is intended. So far from being sedative, they are explosive. The attempt, in the Western provinces of the Roman Empire, to corral the taxpayer and to chain the artisan's son to his father's trade did not keep the economy going; it hastened its collapse. The contrast between the fall of the Roman Empire in the West and Meiji Revolution in Japan illustrates this point. In the nineteenth century, Japan performed an uncommonly difficult feat. Without running into disaster, she transformed herself from being an insulated and would-be frozen world state into becoming one of the many local states of the rapidly moving modern world that she had been keeping at arm's length during the preceding two centuries. How was this Japanese miracle accomplished? There were some Japanese fanatics who, in this crisis in Japan's history, did their worst to bring Japan to ruin by kicking against the pricks; but this was not the reaction of the majority of those Japanese who, at that time, were in positions of power and privilege. The majority had the wisdom to read the signs of the times, and also had the public spirit to accept necessary changes while there was still time to make them peacefully—though, after two centuries of freezing, these necessary changes were revolutionary, and required the sacrifice of personal interests and class interests. The Tokugawa House recognized that its mandate was exhausted, and handed back to the Imperial House, without a struggle, the usurped power that had been won by blood and iron two and a half centuries back. The feudal lords and their retainers voluntarily renounced their social privileges. These privileges had already proved to be illusory, but it needed insight to take the point, and public spirit to act on the insight.

There is surely a lesson here for a future warless world. The lesson is that, if unity and peace have been established, the only way to preserve these precious achievements will be to recognize, and act on, the truth that continuous change is of the essence of human life. To try to halt change is to court an explosion. The constructive way of dealing with the inevitability of change is to make changes voluntarily before they impose themselves. The earlier we take action, the wider will be our range of choice. If we foresee a necessary change soon enough, we shall have some chance of controlling it and of guiding it into channels in which its effects will be, not devastating, but constructive.

This is a lesson for a future society that has achieved a warless world, because it is a lesson for all human beings at all times and in all circumstances. In this new age of atomic weapons, a warless world has become a necessity of human life and a necessary condition for mankind's survival. A policy of accepting and promoting peaceful change is a necessary condition for the maintenance of a warless world.

# IV

## The question of internal change

BY WALTER MILLIS

Staff Director, Center for
the Study of Democratic Institutions

The problem of change and the problem of order are the two horns of a dilemma upon which political thought has been impaled for the past two or three millennia; and it is not suggested that this brief paper can fully resolve it. Yet is is a dilemma which must be faced by those contemplating a world without organized war. It is obvious that it is impossible, as Toynbee puts it, for a government to freeze human life; change is inherent in all political and social institutions. But it is equally obvious that any form of governance is impossible if it allows human life to boil itself away in a completely disorderly chaos. Those who try to imagine a warless world are trying to imagine a special form of world order, or governance, which must nevertheless allow for the disorder, conflict, and change essential to the survival and development of human social and political institutions. They must form some idea of how such change, which throughout history has been so often and so deeply associated with organized war, will continue to come about within the warless order they are trying to envisage. That it will continue to come about is scarcely arguable.

The answer, it seems clear, must turn upon the nature and structure of the warless world order; and ideas about this may differ very widely. The situation which each of the authors in this book has been asked to assume as his starting point—a situation including general disarmament to police-force level; an in-

ternationally controlled police force adequate to its responsibilities, and a "peace-keeping and dispute-settling system" with
at least enough "law" to avert organized war between states—is
insufficiently specific to offer much guidance. The terms are (no
doubt intentionally) so general as to define almost any form of
world order, from a total system of global government to a
situation not so very different from that at which, as a consequence of the nuclear stalemate, we seem already to be arriving. It seems necessary to bring the nature of the assumed
warless order into a clearer focus, and for that it may be helpful
to look more closely at the general problem of law and order,
violence and war.

The complicated struggle among individuals, groups, classes,
communities, or nations for wealth, position and power is inherent in human nature. No system of law and order can eliminate these power struggles; any such system may be regarded as
primarily a means of regulating or structuring them, among those
who are subject to the system, in such a way that they are
resolved with a minimum of physical violence. The relative
justice of the regulation is a highly important support for the
system, but it seems essentially secondary—a by-product, as it
were—to the "order" which the system imposes. There have
been, of course, highly unjust orders which have survived over
long periods and comparatively just orders which have suffered
early collapse. The essential of any system of law and order, just
or unjust, is that it forces the competitive struggles among its
members into other than lethal or violent channels.

In any system of law and order one finds three elements,
which are the mechanisms through which it achieves this result:
A sovereign monopoly of legal force to forbid resort to violence;
a system of general rules (law) defining in generalized terms
the rights, duties, and therefore, the power positions of all involved; a judicial system to apply the general rules in specific
conflicts and to provide in its decisions a generally accepted
alternative to trial by combat or violence. No system of this
kind, of course, is ever perfectly successful. An irreducible minimum of violent crime, usually a certain amount of riot and group
violence, remains under the most developed systems of law and

order. Nor has any such system ever completely inhibited change. It is true that a developed system of law and order has the effect, at any given time, of defining—as it were crystallizing—the power relations of the individuals, groups, and classes subject to it, and that this crystallized legal structure of power may survive after the actual power relationships in the community have changed. But when the actual power structure tends to get out of line with the legal definition, it is, sooner or later, the legal definition which alters, not the newly emerging structure of power.

When the discrepancy between the fact and the form grows too great, such changes may be violent, reflected in great wars on the international stage or bloody revolutions within. But war and violent revolution are by no means the only or the necessary means of adjusting the system of law and order to changes in the underlying power structure. The modern world has recorded immense adjustments of this kind affected by largely, if not wholly, nonviolent means. Nor is it true that these can occur only in those systems which, as in the Western democracies, include formal provision for popular participation in institutional change. Toynbee, in the preceding chapter, cites the abdication of the Tokugawa Shogunate in Japan—at the time anything but a democratic society—and the accompanying political and social revolution, all accomplished with very little violence. Since the death of Stalin, if not before, considerable shifts have plainly been occurring in the power structure both of the Soviet Union itself and among the constituent states of the Communist empire. But the Communist system of law and order (which is no less a system of law and order because it seems to us an unjust one) has accommodated itself to these changes in general without war or revolution. The one violent revolution of importance —that in Hungary—was suppressed by the Soviet police power, thus leaving Communist law and order outwardly intact. But even the ruthlessness with which the "order" was reimposed does not mean that it is perpetually unchangeable. The Hungarian revolt will still make its contribution toward those changes—hopefully nonviolent, but changes in any event—which shifts in the underlying Communist power structure are certain to bring about.

Even the existing international order, "anarchic" as it is commonly assumed to be, has since 1945 adjusted itself to very great changes in the basic power relations of peoples, states, classes, and groups with, on the whole, a rather surprising minimum of war or other violence. Discussions of a new world order usually overlook the fact that we already possess a more highly developed system of international law and order than ever before in history. It is a system not yet reduced to statutory form or fully embodied in treaty undertakings; while its institutional expressions, such as the UN, are still quite rudimentary. It is a system, nevertheless. It is incapable, certainly, of "freezing" the political and social institutions of mankind into any perpetual mold; yet it is currently proving itself adequate to insure that for most peoples, most of the time, the infinitely complex struggle for power is carried on by essentially nonviolent means.

Perhaps two-thirds of the population of the globe lives today under no more than four or five great, stabilized, mutually more or less invulnerable centers of power, of law, and of order—the United States, the Western European democracies, the Soviet Union, China, perhaps India—which appear rather effectively to have excluded violence and bloodshed from their domestic affairs as instruments of practical politics. Each has effectively developed the essentials of a rule of law: a police quite capable of forbidding anything more than merely casual resort to violence; a system of general rules to govern the internal power struggle, and at least some kind of adjudicatory and regulatory system to apply the rules and to offer an alternative to trial by violence which, however imperfect or unjust, will be generally accepted as preferable. These great systems of law and order differ widely in their efficiency, their subtlety, and their sophistication as social organizations. It is difficult, for instance, to find much parallel between the deliberations of the Supreme Court of the United States and the intrigues within the Soviet power elite in the Kremlin, except that both serve the same broad purpose. Each offers an acceptable (or at any rate accepted) alternative to armed violence and rebellion in the settlement of basic power issues. Different as they are, each of these great systems appears to have established its ability to keep order together with enough flexibility to permit necessary change to take place without extremes of violence.

This, at any rate, appears to be the common opinion. No one, for example, can seriously suppose that the United States will remain fixed in perpetuity in the particular mold of political, social, and economic relationships which it had attained in mid-1963. We all look for great changes of one kind or another in the American power structure; but it takes a John Birchoid mentality to imagine that violent revolution either will or can accompany them. Much the same is true of the Western European democracies. But, if one accepts the view of most observers, it is true of the great Communist states as well. The shifting and uncertain power relations between Moscow and Peking are well advertised in the Western press; but no serious student has been rash enough to predict that they will end in a Sino-Soviet war. It is not the likelihood of armed rebellion in China or the U. S. S. R. that impresses most, but its apparent impossibility in the foreseeable future. Two-thirds of the population of the globe already live under reasonably stable systems of law and order, so stable that no one predicts violent revolution or collapse for any of them (unless as a result of another world war), yet not so rigid as to be incapable of necessary change and development.

By whatever paths of blood and misery the world has attained this result, it has attained it; one must recognize its novelty—for it is a phenomenon almost as unprecedented in history as are the nuclear arsenals themselves—as well as its obvious importance to the general problem of world law and order. Unfortunately, much of the remaining third of the global population is less well organized. Southern Asia, Africa, much of Latin America, are being swept by the "revolution of expectations," inordinately complicated by nationalism, by racial and class conflict, by differences between the small educated elite groups with their urban followers and the peasant masses, as well as by the tendency of the great, stable power centers to exploit these difficulties for the advancement of their own power and influences. Speaking very generally, over much of this area the basic power structures (both domestic and international) are in a state of fluidity; it is the problem of the new leaderships not so much to "seize power" as to discover the new bases on which a viable power structure may be erected. What rules (law) are available, whether derived from decisions in the United Nations, from the principles of international law or from domestic constitutional and institutional arrangements, are clearly out of line with the highly complicated actual power relationships. Over much of this area no general rule of "law and order," even a repressive one like that which the Soviet Union has successfully established over its many different peoples and different conflicts of interest, seems possible. And it would appear that a good deal of violence—whether in the savage form that occurred in the Congo or in Algeria, or simply the military *coup d'état* that has, with relatively little bloodshed, interrupted the processes of "democracy" in so many parts of the world—is inevitable. No system of law and order can hope to avert all violence, or dispense "justice" with a hand so even that men, groups, and communities will never seek to "take the law in their own hands." But it is still surprising that so little, not so much, violence and bloodshed has attended the enormous shifts in group, class, and national power relationships which have taken place since 1945.

Such is the situation in which we find ourselves today. We have developed a system of world law and order unprecedented in human experience. It contains no global monopoly of legal force, adequate to forbid violent solutions to nations, classes, communities, and groups, although for the time being the great weapons systems seem to be providing an effective substitute. Change is certainly proceeding as rapidly as most could wish; yet within an order sufficient to permit the vast majority of the world's peoples to live currently at peace and to keep such violence as does continue to occur within tolerable bounds. It is an order sufficient to permit even more, to permit the growth of the web of relationships among the peoples of the world that Robert C. Angell has felicitously called the "interstitial tissue" of global organization. What would be the effect on this general situation of the assumed excision from it of the organized war system?

This is really the central question. All that we have been asked to assume in these chapters is an initial abolition of organized war, with the introduction of whatever (only vaguely specified) institutional arrangements may be necessary to maintain the abolition. How, so far as securing necessary social and political change is concerned, would the resultant warless system differ from the existing one? The easy answer it to say that it would differ very little; but there is an obstacle to the easy answer. That lies in the still obscure but clearly intimate relationship which has existed through most of history between domestic violence and revolution and international violence and war. The two have probably been intermingled in most of the major changes in human systems of law, order, and power organization. Great wars have led to great revolutions; great revolutions have led to great wars. Perhaps the causal relationship was not in fact as simple as this would suggest; but the observation at least inspires an inquiry as to whether, if there are no more great wars, there can be any more great revolutions; or, conversely, if there are to be further great evolutions will not great wars inevitably be revived?

Our presently existing world order seems to be both sufficiently flexible and sufficiently stable to meet the necessities of change without intolerable concomitants of violence. But so did the Atlantic world appear to its inhabitants on the eve of the French Revolution; so did the Western and the Russian imperial world appear on the eve of the First World War. Both the Soviet Union and China today appear to represent stable systems of law and order. But the appearance may prove to be illusory. As power relationships continue to shift within the rigid frameworks of these great societies, it may be that nothing short of violent and bloody rebellion will suffice to break up the old power structures and institute the new.

Revolutionary violence in France after 1789 not only reorganized the domestic power structure; it fractured the international power structure of the time and led on to the first total wars of modern history. Given an initially warless world, a similar violent breakdown of the Russian or Chinese power structures might have similar effects. No presently imaginable system of policed disarmament could deal finally or completely with such a situation. It is hard to picture an international police force endowed with either the physical force or, more importantly, the authority to intervene in a chaotic Russia in order to "restore order." It is easy to imagine the pressures upon the contiguous national police forces to intervene in one way or another in order to preserve their national interests; and to see that these pressures could lead to "escalation," rearmament, and war by processes which the international police would find it difficult to control. All that one can say to this is that perfection is unattainable in this world; no system of politics will infallibly meet all the problems that may arise before it, but that a politics which starts from a universal and policed disarmament has a far better chance of meeting this sort of situation than has one which starts with the system of organized war.

There is the opposite case, often illustrated by the Russian Revolution of 1918, in which it is held that great international wars are necessary to break up encrusted and anachronistic power structures inhibiting human development. That wars have had this effect can hardly be doubted, but that major war is a necessary element in political and social advance is much more dubious. In the usual view, the Russian Revolution actually began with Alexander II's emancipation of the serfs in 1861, a voluntary recognition by the autocracy (not unlike the abdication of the Tokugawa Shogunate) that times were changing and that the legally established power structure in Russia would have to be modified accordingly. The process thereafter continued, haltingly, not without a good deal of violence on the part of government and revolutionaries alike, but rather steadily. Even imperial Russia had within it the potentialities of necessary change; and many believe that the autocracy would have undergone a relatively peaceable "constitutionalization" of the new power relationships—rather as happened in Britain and was happening in Germany—*except* for the First World War. The Russo-Japanese War of 1904–05 no doubt pushed the autocracy along the avenues to modernization; but World War I simply paralyzed and finally destroyed it, leaving it as helpless to promote as it was to resist the change which was overdue. Power passed by default into other and more ruthless hands, which built and imposed a new power structure, at least somewhat more responsive to the realities than the Czarist system had been, though hardly an ideal case of political and social evolution. The First World War, in this view, was not necessary to political and social change in Russia; all that it did was to distort this change into extreme, and generally inefficient, forms.

Organized war and violent domestic revolution have thus been closely associated, historically, in the processes of political and social change. But the exact nature of the association is not too clear; and it is not easy to be dogmatic about the probable effect of the removal of one, organized war, from the global order. One may hazard some guesses. In the absence of international war certain processes of violent internal change could not go on as they have done. Revolutionaries, for example, would have less chance of acquiring small arms, financial and propaganda support from rival outside powers than they have today. At the same time, they would have less to fear from outside intervention. To revert to the eighteenth-century examples, another American Revolution could not count on the assistance rendered by France as a strategic move in her war with Britain; another French Revolution would not have to face the coalition of powers which, in defence of the *ancien régime,* sought to crush the original. It is not easy to strike a plausible balance between such possibilities; but so far as the present great organized power centers are concerned, it seems reasonable to predict that the abolition of organized war among them would not seriously affect the problem of necessary change. After all, at the end of World War I, the Western Allies attempted to intervene with armed force in the Russian revolutionary situation, in a way they could not do in a world disarmed by assumption. Their ill-success at least suggests that the presence or absence of national armaments would not greatly affect such basic reorganizations of the power structure as were then taking place.

Perhaps the real question lies not with the great and relatively stabilized power systems, but with the less organized areas. How far will a warless world order try to limit the more sporadic disorder and violence that one must expect here? In a generally disarmed world, one may expect the simple absence of the hypertrophied weapons systems to supply an adequate equivalent for a global monopoly of legal force. The want of the necessary weapons systems will generally forbid resort to violence by any of the great power centers. (The argument, it must be remembered, is based on the assumption of a situation in which these weapons systems have been *voluntarily* laid aside and destroyed.) But with the survival everywhere of national police forces, there will be no lack of at least light weapons in the world, accessible to bold or desperate men and to their followers. Riot and mob violence, the more organized use of such weapons as plastic bombs, even still more highly organized forms of guerrilla war, will still be possible. The military *coup d'état* will still be possible through the manipulation of the national police. (Indeed, most of the "military" forces which have participated in such affairs have amounted to little more than what one would expect the national police in a warless world to be.) How far will a warless order, through its international police force, attempt to control all these forms of residual violence?

It seems improbable that the attempt will go very far. The assumed elimination of major organized war must, after all, eliminate the one great danger in current minor war and violence —the danger of escalation into a Great Power conflict. It seems evident that the warless order must have not merely an international but a supranational (that is, veto-free) police force to control disarmament and to ensure that rearmament does not take place. But a supranational, veto-free police can take on reality only as its empowerment (authority) as well as the physical force at its disposal are strictly limited to those requisite for its police functions. It is difficult to envisage an international or supranational police force as a great army, capable of coercing the states which must support it and overawing the national police forces which they will retain. One sees this force rather as comparable to the American Federal Bureau of Investigation, which wields very great power within the American system, but does so precisely because its weapons are of negligible importance and its empowerment strictly limited. The FBI obviously could not wage a successful armed battle with any state or municipal police force. It has other means of ensuring its power in state and municipal police circles; and it seems obvious that the real power of the supranational police force vis-à-vis the remaining national police forces with which it must work will rest on similar bases.

The concept of an "international police power" has a long, though generally unfortunate history. Experience seems to demonstrate that while some power of the kind is necessary to avert extremes of savagery, violence, and irresponsibility, it can succeed in this much only if it refrains from itself trying to settle or decide the power struggles out of which the violence arises. One may compare the UN "police action" in Korea with that which it was driven by circumstance to take in Palestine and the Congo. The attempt in the first case was to intervene in a major power struggle, and it ended, as probably it could only have ended, in a fairly major international war. In Palestine and the Congo the attempt has been to limit the savagery so far as possible without authority to decide the power struggles involved. It seems probable that the patterns on which the supranational police in a warless world order would tend to develop are to be found in the Congo, not in Korea. For its problems would, in a real sense, be police and not military problems.

Perhaps what was first advanced as the easy answer is the right answer as well. Assuming the abstraction of the organized war system, the political and social institutions reflecting the underlying power organization of the world, of its peoples, states, classes, communities, and groups would continue to grow and change in about the same way they are now doing, but without the corroding and overwhelming fear of catastrophe which today complicates and distorts every real problem of international politics.

# V

## Peaceful international change

BY ARTHUR LARSON

Director, World Rule of Law Center,
Duke University, and former Director,
U.S. Information Agency

When it is said that solving the problem of peaceful change is an absolute condition precedent to achieving a warless world, what kind of change is meant? The task becomes clearer if we identify three main kinds of change: internal political change and revolution; change in international political relations; and change in the economic, social, educational, technical, and living standards of the poorer nations in relation to the wealthier.

Internal change and revolution were the principal concern of the preceding chapter. The author's conclusion was that any international organization and armed force could not and should not go far in attempting to control the residual violence that will continue to play a part in readjusting human rights within countries, particularly in the less organized areas. Indeed, no other conclusion is possible if we are to retain the cardinal principle of international relations, which is noninterference in the purely internal affairs of other countries. The proper role of the international community in a disarmed world under law would be first, to see that outsiders did not foment or assist internal revolution, and second to intervene with police or other necessary action whenever an apparently internal conflict threatened international peace. There is already ample precedent for this principle, since it was precisely these two functions that the United Nations undertook in the Congo.

When we turn to international as distinguished from internal change, the question whether change can be reconciled with warlessness is presented in its starkest form. As one confronts this assignment, one has moments in which even to make the attempt seems to betray an arrogance bordering on the supernatural. We place two facts side by side. The first fact is that the world is passing through an era of upheaval, revolution, and volcanic ferment without historic parallel. Hundreds of millions of people whose societies have been static for centuries are lurching into the twentieth century, and wholesale revisions of political and economic relationships are occurring around the globe. Militant nationalism, aggressive communism, fanatical regionalism, explosive racialism, and emotional anticolonialism are in full play all round us, demanding quick and drastic change. We superimpose on this seething situation the second fact, which is that throughout human history war has always been the ultimate arbiter and vehicle of change. How then can anyone—at this time of all times—seriously talk of removing war completely from the human scene? For removed completely it must be, so far as international disputes are concerned. We do not here have open to us the option—as in the case of internal conflict—of tolerating a moderate amount of war. Even a small international war under disarmament conditions would be intolerable, because of the well-known proclivity of small wars to grow into big wars.

The reason we must make the attempt is clear and unanswerable: we have no choice. Extrapolation of the present directions taken by the Great Powers (again consulting history as a guide) leads inexorably to disaster of incomprehensible dimensions.

Before we despair too quickly in the presence of this problem of change without war, let us look at a change of somewhat comparable magnitude that was indeed achieved without the equivalent of war. This is the change which the politically and economically downtrodden masses of working people achieved during the past century or so in England, the United States, and much of Western Europe. Karl Marx and many others looked about at the wretched mill and mine workers—some of whom hardly ever saw daylight because they entered the pit before dawn and emerged after dark—and concluded that nothing short of bloody revolution would suffice to accomplish the tremendous change that would give these workers their full rights as human beings. However, the workers in these countries in the hundred years which followed did not resort to large-scale revolutionary violence and did in fact achieve a revolutionary change in their economic and political status.

Always recognizing the limitations of any such domestic-international analogy, one may still profitably begin by asking the question: how was this revolutionary change achieved without class war?

There is no single answer. A number of forces were simultaneously at work, and the significant fact for present purposes is that these forces have striking counterparts on the present international scene.

The first thing to note is that, while this change was brought about without large-scale organized violence, it was not brought about without pressure. We may as well face one fact at the outset: we are not trying to get rid of struggle in human or international relationships; the problem is to keep inevitable struggle from taking the form of organized war. One key to our problem is this question: are there available forms of pressure for achieving change that are at the same time nonviolent and yet sufficiently effective to make ultimate resort to organized violence unnecessary?

Of course there was some violence in the story of labor. There were shootings, killings, and beatings in connection with some of the more bitter strikes, but these must by any fair test be regarded as only marginal to the main pressures that brought about the change. Central to this nonviolent pressure was the organization of strong unions. In their hands, the right to strike, boycott, picket, and bargain collectively became a formidable economic weapon.

A rough counterpart to these pressures exercised by working-men is the strength possessed by the newer and poorer countries because of the competition of the Great Powers for their support and friendship. There are many reasons for this competition—economic, strategic, and political. Whatever its source, this ability of the smaller countries to apply pressure by the granting or withholding of their favor is as much a lever for peaceful changes as the strike and boycott. Indeed, as the newer countries continue to learn to use this power collectively—as workingmen did—its impact will markedly increase.

The other principal nonviolent pressure is that of political power in a form that can be tangibly expressed. In the story of the amelioration of workers' rights, this took the form of obtaining full voting rights without restrictions based on property ownership.

The counterpart to this kind of nonviolent pressure on the international scale is the one-nation one-vote principle in the United Nations General Assembly. This principle has frequently been criticized because of the apparent illogic of conferring the same voting power on a tiny new nation in Africa as on the United States or France. There was a time when similar arguments were heard about the illogic of giving the same vote to a propertyless laborer as to a highly educated man of affairs. In any event, the one-nation one-vote principle is firmly established in the General Assembly, and the General Assembly is increasingly taking actions of major importance, such as the authorization of the United Nations force in the Middle East and the resolution pursuant to which the invasion of Suez was stopped. This voting power in itself is a substantial source of pressure which the smaller and poorer nations are finding quite effective in gaining change without physical violence.

These enhanced strengths of workers—and of small new nations—might not be an adequate substitute for force if, from the other side, there had been encountered an implacable hostility to change which in its turn was prepared to use force. But paralleling this increase in strength was a change in the attitudes and policies of employers, a factor entirely left out of account in Marx's calculations. The phrase most often used to describe this new attitude was "enlightened self-interest." The employer gradually discovered that he prospered more under an economy of high wages, high purchasing power, universal education, and worker security. The classical capitalist, like the classical colonist, may perhaps have thought that the greatest prosperity lay in wringing out of the worker or the colony as much selfish gain as possible—although these classical types may have been less prevalent than they have been pictured. Now the enlightened industrial country begins to realize that an independent and prospering small nation which becomes a good customer is a greater source of prosperity than the same area in the form of a colony.

The most important change in economic thought contributing to this possibility of peaceful change was the discovery that the way to raise everyone's standard of living was to achieve greater production for all to share. Marx, like most economists prior to John Stuart Mill, was obsessed with the matter of distribution. To him the economic problem seemed to be one of dealing with a fixed supply of wealth, which must be taken away from one class and given to another. Abraham Lincoln, at about the same time, adumbrated the modern theory when he said: "Let not him who is houseless pull down the house of another, but let him labor diligently and build one for himself."

This simple concept—that everyone comes out ahead when there are two houses where only one existed before—has now been enthusiastically taken over by the Soviet Union, which, in disregard of Marxian economics, concentrates its energies in an almost frantic preoccupation with increase in production, accompanied by challenges to the rest of the world to engage in production races.

The inevitable concomitant of emphasis on productivity, on the international as well as on the internal economic front, is that, in the self-interest of the more industrialized countries, markets must be built up through the bolstering of the prosperity and purchasing power of those who are now poor.

In addition, just as enlightened employers and societies translated their new concept of self-interest into concrete programs, such as social insurance, free public education, and wage-and-hour legislation, so the wealthier countries now can forestall the temptation to violence by anticipating and actively helping to provide for the acute needs of the poorer countries, through stabilization of commodity prices and markets, and economic, educational, and technical aid.

In addition, quite apart from self-interest, one can without sentimentality and with perfect accuracy say that there have been many individuals and many countries which have been motivated to contribute to improving the lot of less fortunate people by ethical, humanitarian, and religious considerations that are seldom spoken of for fear of inviting the ridicule of the cynical. This element cannot be measured in international conduct, any more than one could measure the relative contribution of conscience in the changed policies of employers over the past century; yet it is unquestionably a real factor in such epoch-making vehicles of change as the voluntary liquidation of the British Empire and the American program of economic and technical aid.

It may be suggested, then, that when increased nonviolent pressures for change became increasingly available to those most ardently seeking change, and when those in a position to facilitate the change became increasingly imbued with the good sense and good will needed to impel them to help rather than resist change in the mutual interest, the prospect of achieving international change in a warless world begins to come within the bounds of reality.

Fundamental to the whole concept of peaceful change is the principle that real change can most effectively take place within a framework of law. At first glance, there may seem to be a paradox in this statement. Certainly one has often heard representatives of the newer countries explain their coolness toward the rule of law in international affairs with the statement: "The law preserves the *status quo;* we want change." The tragic fallacy in this attitude toward law is the notion that true change comes about by changing laws. The historical fact is that most important change is achieved when there is a reliable environment of law. By contrast, when there is no such reliable environment of law, stagnation almost invariably sets in, and the result is not change but actual regression. Contrast, for example, the breathtaking changes in the era of Roman commercial law, the Mercantile period, or the modern period of Western Europe and America, with the deadly economic paralysis that characterized much of the Middle Ages. If a trader can make a contract in Bergen, Norway, knowing that it will be honored in Genoa, quite a different kind of world develops than one in which a binding contract could not be made even with the person living on the next manor.

So, before anyone says, "The law preserves the *status quo;* I want change," let him remember that *one rule of law, the rule that agreements must be kept, has caused more change in the world than all the governmental appropriations and expropriations of history.*

The impatience of the newer countries to achieve change at a forced-draft pace is understandable and must be reckoned with; but fortunately most of them are gradually learning this lesson. If a new country insists that it prefers the short-term policy of disregarding legal rights in order to have the elbow room to expropriate foreign investments and industries, it may at first think that it is thereby promoting change in the most effective way. In most cases, however, the value of the expropriated industry is trivial compared with the value of private investment that would pour into that country over a long period of years if reasonable assurance of safety were provided by stable legal framework. We are now witnessing in country after country the "morning after," with new countries looking at their expropriated tea plantations, refineries, and factories, run down and floundering for lack of necessary skills, capital, markets, and experience —and with disillusionment taking the place of the high hopes for a quickly transformed economy. A *New Yorker* cartoon summed up the situation, showing one bearded character glumly saying to another, as they sit in an office in a converted palace: "Remember the good old days when there was still something to expropriate?" A factory can be expropriated; economic development cannot. Reserving the right to kick holes at will in the law brings less real change than occurs when the mighty drives of economic interest come into full play because of an orderly legal environment.

Certainly the changing of laws may play a part in the over-all achievement of change in the world, but it is a minor part. We are often told that the fatal flaw in our present world organization is that it does not have the power to pass binding legislation and thus to change existing law when existing law becomes a drag upon progress or a source of injustice. And yet, see what has happened even in the absence of this legislative power. During the lifetime of the United Nations, there has occurred the most rapid and wide-scale series of changes in political relationships for any comparable period in history. The colonial system has been almost completely dismantled. Some fifty new countries have come into existence. In some instances there was indeed bloodshed. For the most part, however, and particularly more recently, this change has come about with surprisingly little physical conflict. As John Gunther wrote in *Think* magazine for January, 1962: "With a minimum of violence twenty-nine countries [of Africa], some of them primitive in the extreme, have reached national freedom . . . and in the majority of countries the amount of disorder that resulted was less than what occurs in Chicago on a noisy Saturday night."

If we look again at our initial division of international change into political change on the one hand and economic, social, and related change on the other, we must concede that the larger part of the process of changing basic international political relationships has already been put behind us. Some difficult colonial problems remain, and new political relationships in the form of federations or other groupings will no doubt have to be worked out where the small new countries are not viable units. The larger part of the remaining task of change has to do with standards of living, populations, education, health, and all the other factors that separate the poverty-stricken areas of the world from the goals they are setting for themselves. As to this kind of change, the lesson of history is eloquent and emphatic. It cannot be achieved by bloodshed and war; it cannot be achieved by disorder and lawlessness; it can be achieved and will best be achieved in a world in which the powerful human drives for accomplishment, invention, exploration, and construction are allowed fullest expression because of the guarantees implicit in the rule of law, and in which the pressures for changing legal rights and relationships as necessary are channeled into orderly courses, through an international organization expressing the conscience and good sense of the world community.

# VI

## The economic implications of warlessness

BY KENNETH E. BOULDING

Professor of Economics and Co-director
of the Center for Research on Conflict Resolution,
University of Michigan

The basic assumption of this volume is that models of a world
social system can be constructed that have the property of warlessness. Since there may be a number of such systems, it is important to find which of the alternatives is the "cheapest," in the
sense of being the easiest to get to and involving the least sacrifice
of existing values. The gains of warlessness in these days are so
enormous that, even if the costs were fairly high, they would still
be worth incurring. However, it is the fear of the costs of warlessness which mainly inhibits man's movement toward a system
of this kind. If we can show that the costs are unqualifiedly less
than the gains, it would undermine the fear which holds back
the movement of mankind toward peace, which is the fear of
"peace at any price." This is only acceptable if we regard the
costs of war as infinite. Only a few people have ever regarded
war in this light, and mankind up to now has not regarded warlessness as worth its costs. As the image spreads, however, of
the rising costs of war and the declining costs of peace, a point
will certainly come at which the search for a warless-world social
system will no longer seem utopian, and will become a sober
search for "peace at least cost."

As we try to construct models of a warless social system, the
economic sector of the social system makes its impact at two
points. We have first of all the problem of the difficulties which
warlessness might create for the economic system itself; this is

the set of problems which is usually associated with the term "economics of disarmament." The second set of problems relates to the strains which the economic sector of the social system places upon the institutions of warlessness. This is a set of problems which is frequently referred to as the economic causes of war. If there are forces arising out of the economic system which make for war, obviously, the institutions of warlessness have to deal with them.

The first set of questions, relating to the impact of warlessness on the world economy, is perhaps the easiest to deal with. The world war economy has been estimated at something between 110 and 120 billion dollars a year. A little over a third of this may be attributed to the United States, and a little under a third to the Soviet Union, and the rest to all other countries put together. This, of course, is a major sector of the world economy, and the problem of transferring it to peaceful uses is formidable, though by no means insuperable. The world war economy is roughly equal in magnitude to the total income of the poorer half of the world's population. Even at that, however, the war economy today represents only 10 per cent of the American gross national product, probably about 15 per cent of the product of the Soviet Union, and about 5 per cent of the product of most other countries. We can perhaps visualize the real significance of these magnitudes, if we reflect that in the United States and probably also in the Soviet Union, the total war economy is roughly equivalent to three or four years' growth of the total economy; that is, suppose that we were able by waving a magic wand to turn the whole war industry into civilian uses overnight, all of a sudden the civilian economy would be where it is going to be in 1966 or 1967. For the United States this would mean a little extra luxury for the masses, a little more leeway in cleaning up existing pockets of poverty, in improving education and health services, and so on. For the Soviet Union this would mean a very real advance toward comfort; it would mean consumer goods, household appliances, better housing, and the lifting of the burden of drabness that spreads like a grimy pall over Soviet society. For the poor countries, however, in the broad belt of human misery that wraps the earth around its equator, the turning of the world war industry into civilian uses may well make the difference between life and death, between advancing into the new world of science, technology, and relative affluence on the one hand, and falling back into misery, starvation, and anarchy on the other. Even though there will be no necessity for the rich countries to turn the war industry into the support of the poor ones, the mere fact that the resources released from the war industry will be so great, relative to the income of the poor countries, means that the resources which will be available to aid them in making their great transition into the modern age will be larger almost by an order of magnitude than they are now, and it will be surprising if this availability cannot be organized and actualized.

The problems involved in the economics of warlessness may be divided into those which involve the process of transition, and those which involve the operation of the economy in the final stage. The most obvious problem of the transition is the problem of conversion—that is, the traditional one of beating swords into ploughshares, missile factories into space exploration, and generals into corporation executives. This problem often looms large in popular imagination, because it is essentially an immediate, short-run problem. If other conditions are right, however, this is probably the least difficult of the problems. It is curious how, in the United States, we remember the fact that it took Hitler to take us out of the great Depression, and that it was not until rearmament started that the unemployment of the thirties disappeared. For some reason, however, we seem to have forgotten the great disarmament of 1945–1946, when in a single year, we converted to civilian uses a total war industry equal to $2\frac{1}{2}$ times what we have at present. We did this, furthermore, without at any time having more than 3 per cent unemployment. It must be pointed out, of course, that conditions in the economy were highly favorable. Consumers were extraordinarily liquid, as a result of the methods of war finance. There was a large accumulated deficiency of consumer goods, and hence there was no problem of aggregate demand, which, indeed, was overfull, and gave us an inflation.

The thing to remember, however, is that given these circum-

stances the actual problem of conversion presented surprisingly
few difficulties. In this respect the American economy is astonishingly flexible. The Russian economy likewise has all the
instrumentalities for achieving a conversion of this kind. It is a
nice question, which I am glad to leave to the Sovietologists,
whether the problem would be more or less difficult in the Soviet
Union than in the United States. It is certainly arguable that the
problem of conversion might be more difficult in the Soviet
Union, because the Soviet economy has not had any experience
of this kind, and because, owing to its controlled nature, it has
never had to face the problem of adaptability in the way that a
market economy does. This, however, is not a point of great
importance, for there is no reason to suppose that the Soviet
economy is incapable of achieving basic conversion.

The problem of operating a world economy under a condition
of warlessness is more difficult and also more obscure than the
problem of conversion. There is little doubt, for instance, that the
*size* of the war economy in the United States has assisted in
stabilizing the whole economy in the last fifteen years, even
though the *fluctuations* in the war economy have been themselves
a destabilizer. The reason for this has little to do with the fact
that it is a war economy; it is simply that it is a government
economy. The government sector of the United States economy,
for instance, is about 20 per cent of the gross national product,
10 per cent of which is civilian, and 10 per cent military. The
stabilizing effect on the private economy arises mainly from the
size of the tax system which is necessary to finance military expenditure. The deductible-at-source income tax is a particularly
valuable automatic stabilizer. If inflation gets under way and
money incomes begin to rise, larger numbers of people begin to
get into the upper income brackets, and income tax collections
rise much more sharply than income. This leads to budget surplus, which removes money from the private sector of the economy and so checks the inflation. If a deflation happens so that
money incomes decline, people get out of the upper income
brackets and out of the tax brackets altogether, income tax
collections decline sharply, the Federal budget exhibits a deficit
which increases the money stock in private hands, and hence

checks the deflation. In the absence of military expenditure the Federal sector of the American economy is astonishingly small; in real terms, apart from transfer payments, it absorbs only 1 to 2 per cent of the gross national product. In order to maintain the stabilizing properties of the existing tax system there would almost certainly have to develop a more sophisticated attitude at both state and Federal levels toward the nature and functions of the tax system. Unfortunately, the level of economic education is so low in the United States that it is somewhat doubtful whether this degree of sophistication could be obtained, at least in the near future. The problem here is educational and psychological rather than economic, but it is still a severe one. This is, however, a problem which is not peculiar to the economics of disarmament. As we have noted before, the problem which the United States economy faces as a result of its own economic growth is almost of the same order of magnitude as those presented by disarmament. The problem of maintaining full employment is one we must solve anyway; disarmament may make the solution a little more difficult; but if we can solve it without disarmament, it is pretty clear that we can solve it with disarmament.

The problem of maintaining economic stability or full employment may, of course, also plague us in the transition, and if we do not maintain full employment in the transition the problem of conversion itself becomes much more difficult; the greater the general volume of unemployment, the more the economy tends to freeze up at all points, and the more difficult all adjustments become. We may have to face the fact, therefore, that in the transition we may need to maintain a certain degree of inflationary pressure on the monetary side, together with some form of price and wage control. This is not acceptable except as a transition measure, since up to now we have devised no methods of controlling the general level of prices and wages which do not involve us in insuperable long-range difficulties on the administrative side. As a temporary expedient, however, it is possible, and the easiest recipe for achieving a smooth transition from a war to a peace economy would be to combine a sizeable budget deficit with temporary price and wage control. Unfortunately, the political acceptability of this particular recipe is low. It is very hard to convince people, for instance, that a decline in government expenditure ought to be accompanied with an even larger decline in government receipts, so that we actually run a deficit at a time when expenditure is cut back sharply. If, however, the transition is presented as a crisis to be overcome, and if the political leadership is wise and forthright and is able to do an educational job on the American people, the political and psychological difficulties should not be insuperable.

The last problem of a warless economy is whether such an economy would maintain the rate of economic growth which the war economy has created. From the point of view of human welfare, the war economy has not been entirely wasted, because it is almost the only part of the economic system where extravagance in research and development is allowable. An unusually large proportion of resources have been devoted to research and development in this area, and even though this has resulted in virtually destroying the stability of the military system, the results have spilled over into the civilian economy with striking consequences in some fields. Thus it is possible that we would not have had the jet airplane by this time if it had not been for the research and development in the military sector. It can be argued cogently that the primary military emphasis in research and development has in fact distorted the growth of knowledge and the movement of technology, and it can hardly be denied that we would be much better off today, as a world society, if we had devoted to the means of life and happiness the intellectual resources which we have devoted to the means of death and destruction. Here again, the problem is psychological and political, rather than economic. There are no economic reasons why the Congress of the United States should not appropriate to the intellectual effort on the behalf of economic growth the same kind of resources which it now appropriates to research and development in the military sector. If this were the case, we need have no qualms about whether disarmament would reduce the rate of economic growth. The point must be mentioned, however, because these psychological and political conditions are among the major determinants of the results of changes in the economic system. The general conclusions would seem to be that in the capitalist world the economic problems of adjustment to warlessness would be real, but not insuperable, and that their solution may require some adjustments in psychological and political attitudes, and perhaps some minor changes in political and economic institutions; but that really major changes in the nature of the system are not required.

I speak with less knowledge of the Soviet Union and the Socialist camp. It is possible that here the short-run problems are easier, and the long-run problems are harder, from their own point of view, which presumably stresses the maintenance of the kind of society which they now have. The problem of overall stability of the economy is perhaps easier in a Socialist than in a capitalist country, though we must beware of the delusion that just because there is a plan, it must be fulfilled. The errors, disasters, and the consequent economic fluctuations in the Socialist economies have at least been of the same order of magnitude as the fluctuations of the capitalist economies. Nevertheless, because of the control which the Socialist society has over its own price system, as well as over its monetary system, the problem of combining individual freedom with social control, which is often so severe in the market-oriented society, can be solved by the simple expedient of eliminating some of the freedom. One wonders, however, about the long-run consequences of disarmament and development in Socialist countries, simply from the point of view of the impact of the rise of affluence on the desire for freedom. Disarmament will enable the Socialist societies to rise to affluence more rapidly, if they are going to rise at all; this is particularly true of the Soviet Union, and also, one suspects, of the Eastern European countries. Even though the notorious inefficiencies of Socialist agriculture place a certain ceiling on the development of these countries, pending some change in ideology, there seems to be no reason why they should not advance in industry, especially with the advent of automation, to the point where something like a middle-class standard of consumer goods will spread fairly widely over the society. The general introduction of the automobile, for instance, will have a profound effect not only on the social habits of the people but even on their ways of thought, and one wonders how far a puritan and collectivist ideology can withstand the introduction of the automobile on a large scale, in view of the almost inevitably individualistic style of life which it engenders. However, these are speculations which should not be taken too seriously. Certainly in the short run, the problem of adapting the Socialist society to warlessness is no more difficult than that of adapting a market society, and may even be easier. In both cases the problems are real but solvable.

The impact of disarmament on the poor countries, whether capitalist or Socialist, can hardly help being favorable, as we have already noticed. The military establishments of these countries divert resources from desperately needed investment in roads, schools, etc., and there is no doubt that disarmament will increase the probability that a poor country will be able to make the transition to the steady upward growth in riches. It must be pointed out, though, that even if the probability of success in development is increased it is not thereby necessarily increased to unity. The problems of the transition, especially for the poor overpopulated countries such as India and China, are so great that even with the resources released from disarmament there is a real possibility that they may not be able to make the transition, because of their inability to restrain their population increase. The case of China is particularly dubious owing to the failure of socialized agriculture noted earlier. We can easily visualize a situation in China, even with complete disarmament, in which the rapid growth of population outstrips the ability of the collectivized agriculture to increase the food supply, but in which the level of organization of the society is high enough to distribute the meager supplies fairly equal and so to prevent actual famines. Under these circumstances, the society might go on getting hungrier and hungrier until its development is ground to a stop for sheer lack of human energy and calories. Disarmament does little or nothing to solve this problem, not only because the resources released by disarmament tend to be in industry rather than in agriculture, but also because disarmament by itself does not solve the problem of the unrestricted growth of population.

In a warless world, therefore, it is all the more important that a solution to the problem of control of population be found.

This brings us to the currently unfashionable question of the economic causes of war. In our model of the warless world, this resolves itself into the question whether strains arising from the economic system of the world are likely to endanger the institutions of warlessness. This, of course, is not quite the same question as to whether wars in the past had economic causes, but the two questions are clearly related.

Without doubt there have been wars in the past which were closely related to economic conditions. We may think of war as a situation which arises when one organized threat system is confronted with another organized threat system. An organized threat system—for example, a king and his army—obviously has important economic aspects. One can indeed regard ancient civilization, especially a civilization based on slavery, as primarily organized by a threat system of which war soon becomes an intrinsic part, because threats will not be believed unless they are occasionally carried out. But with the development of true exchange and of societies which are based on exchange, the role of the threat system becomes less and less important economically, because exchange is a much more powerful organizer than threats. In the long run, for instance, slave labor does not seem to be able to compete with free labor, in spite of the fact that the free labor usually had to be paid more than its maintenance. I suspect that this is because of the "negative-sum" aspects of the threat system, which if carried out, makes everybody worse off; as compared with the "positive-sum" aspects of exchange, which if carried out, makes everybody better off.

I would regard the economic causes of war, therefore, as only of fundamental importance in primitive economies which are based upon threat systems. In developed economies, as Norman Angell pointed out almost fifty years ago, war is a poor investment, and the more advanced the economy becomes, the poorer —relative to other forms of investment—war becomes. We can observe this by the most casual inspection of Europe, where the countries which have stayed home and minded their own business, like the Scandinavian countries, have done much better economically than countries which have maintained large empires, like Portugal, and in earlier days, Spain. If resources are invested wisely, it is almost true to say that we can get 100 dollars out of nature for every dollar we can squeeze out of man, and the pay-offs to internal development are much greater than those to imperialism and military adventure. The only other case for imperialism, on economic grounds, is that by J. A. Hobson and Lenin, that for a developed, capitalist country foreign investment is necessary in order to preserve full employment at home. The development of the skills of economic stabilization have undermined whatever validity this argument may once have had. Even in its heyday the argument was not a very good one, if only because of the fact that, for the most part, foreign investors tended to do as well or even better in those countries which were not politically dominated by their native land. Thus, British investors did as well in Argentina as they did in India, if not better. These problems are complex and need much further study, but on the whole, one comes down on the side of the classical economists, who believed, in effect, that trade was a substitute for war, and hoped optimistically that with the universal spread of free trade the causes of war would largely disappear.

Even though war as an investment may be shown to be unprofitable, this still does not answer the question whether strains arising out of the war economy would not threaten the institutions of warlessness. War is not always or even usually a rational phenomenon. We do not go to war in the way we make an investment. We go to war because we are angry and frustrated or threatened, or because in general the threat system has gotten out of hand. In the warless world there will unquestionably be strains rising out of the economic system with which the institutions of warlessness will have to deal, simply because these strains will provide a temptation to violence and to the organization of violence. When a group of people perceive a threat, they are strongly tempted to organize a counterthreat, and this is the kind of system which frequently ends in war. We must ask, therefore, what are the elements in the world economic system which will cause groups of people to perceive threats to themselves.

These perceptions, of course, may be illusions; there may be no real threat, but this does not matter. As long as a threat is perceived, it is likely to impose strains on warlessness.

In a brief article one cannot deal with all the economic situations which are likely to be perceived as a threat; we can only hope to classify some of them. In the first place, differential rates of expansion, either of population, or of an economy as a whole, may be perceived, by those whose rate of expansion is smaller, as a threat. We see this happening, for instance, in the racial clashes in British Guiana and the potential difficulties in Trinidad, as a result of the differential fertility of the East Indian and the Negro groups. We see cases where the existence of a minority or of some heterogeneity in the social structure is perceived as a threat to a desired homogeneity. The most extreme example of this was Hitler's treatment of the Jews in Germany, but we see something of the same thing happening on a much smaller scale with the Tamils in Ceylon, the landlords in China, the Kulaks in the Soviet Union, and the Communists in the United States. The degree of threat perception which is involved in heterogeneity is perhaps a psychological rather than an economic phenomenon. Nevertheless, it may have economic roots. The disaster of Hitler, for instance, would have been less probable if so many Germans had not perceived the Jews as growing richer more rapidly than themselves, whether this perception had any basis in fact or not. We come up with a general principle, therefore, that differential growth produces strain. The extent of the strain, however, is not necessarily proportionate to the extent of the differential growth. We have many examples in history in which differential growth has been absorbed with relative ease by society. The less mobility there is between groups, however, and the more groups perceive themselves as fundamentally different and unrelated to others, the more likely is differential growth to produce strain. The institutions of warlessness will have to deal with this problem in some way; how, we do not yet know. Here is an area of research of the utmost importance, and one which has been shockingly neglected.

A question which is related to the above is whether one of the conditions of warlessness in the world as a whole is free migration and free trade. The experience of the United States, and indeed of other countries with civil war, is an indication that the absence of barriers to migration and trade is not in itself a sufficient condition of warlessness. It may well be that a certain amount of restriction of migration and trade may even assist the maintenance of stable peace; the relation between Canada and the United States, for instance, for almost a hundred and fifty years, is a demonstration that warlessness in the real sense can exist between two states, even when there are substantial barriers both to trade and migration, provided that these barriers are not felt to be a threat so great as to initiate military countermeasures. The problem is one of great difficulty. Free migration, for instance, may lead to some part of the world continuously exporting poverty along with its population to the rest. Thus, if one country refuses to control its population growth while the rest of the world achieves this control, it has no right to insist on free migration, even though any sudden cutting off of migration will certainly be regarded as a threat and will create strains. Changes in restrictions on migration and trade are much more likely to create strain than the mere existence of these restrictions, and it may well be that the institutions of warlessness may have to include some institution for moderating the rate of change of restrictions; this may be more important than getting rid of the restrictions altogether.

The above paragraph implies, of course, that a world in stable peace must come to terms eventually with the problem of population expansion as a whole. Eventually there must be a reasonably stable world population, or *any* institution will break down. The long-run institutions of warlessness, therefore, must include the institutions of world-population control, whatever these are going to be. Fortunately, we have a few decades to create these institutions, for we certainly do not know what they would look like at present.

Strains may be placed upon peace not only by the perception of increasing differences among groups, but also by a perception of an absolute worsening of the condition of a single group—that is, if a group of people who have some self-consciousness of themselves as a group perceive that their position today is worse

than it was sometime ago. And if, consequently, they are afraid
that this worsening of their condition may persist, they will perceive this situation as a generalized threat to their continued welfare and existence. A generalized threat, however, has a constant tendency to pass over into the perception of a particular
threat from some other group whether inside or outside the group
which feels itself threatened. This is the familiar phenomenon of
the scapegoat. Thus there seems little doubt that the Great Depression of the thirties had a good deal to do with the rise of
national socialism in Germany.

A worsening of economic conditions may be caused, for instance, by climatic or physical changes which seem to be outside man's physical control, such as drought, pestilence, crop
failures, and so on. In capitalist societies it may be due to deflation, as in the 1930s, which also at the same time seemed to
be an almost unconscious natural force outside man's control.
In Socialist societies it can be due to mistakes in planning, as in
the great collectivization disaster in the Soviet Union in the
1930s. The worsening may also be due to war itself, as innumerable occasions in the history of man can testify. It is not the
actual cause of the worsening, however, which is significant from
the point of view of the strains which it places upon peace; it
is the perception of these causes. The reaction of people and
groups to a perceived experience depends on the view of the
world; it depends, that is, on the image of the social and physical
system in which they live. If it is believed that disasters are caused
by the anger of the gods, a society will undertake religious enterprises, such as sacrifices, in order to ward off or placate this
anger. If a society believes that disaster is due to its own sins,
efforts will be made to repent and atone.

Unfortunately, however, one of the lines of least resistance
under these circumstances is the belief that disaster is usually
caused by the malevolence of other groups either within the
society, such as witches, Jews, or Communists, or outside the
society in the form of other nations. Under these circumstances,
any worsening of conditions from whatever cause is likely to
produce an increase in tensions and an increased probability of
war. The maintenance of stable peace, therefore, probably re-

quires that all societies and subgroups within the world society have a sufficiently realistic image of the social system in which they are placed so that the true causes of any worsening of conditions can be identified, and internal steps can be taken to remedy the situation. Thus, the more successful societies are at solving their internal problems, the smaller will be the strains that are placed on the fabric of world peace. If capitalist societies can prevent depressions and if Socialist societies can prevent major mistakes in planning, the problem of maintaining stable peace will be much easier.

There is an implicit assumption in the above paragraph which may be questioned by some readers—that is, that a world in stable peace is conceivable which is divided into capitalist and Socialist societies. It is a deep strand in the national mythology of the United States that a nation cannot survive half-slave and half-free, or that more generally, two diverse social systems cannot coexist within the same political framework. It is but a step from this argument to argue that the world cannot survive at stable peace if it is half Socialist and half capitalist; that these two social systems are so incompatible that either one must destroy the other or some new synthesis must be found which encompasses them both. If this is true the outlook for mankind is dark indeed, for there seems to be no way in which one system can conquer the other except by a disastrous nuclear war, and at the moment at least any synthesis seems to be far off, though there is some hope that each system is moving in the direction which will bring the systems closer together. If the only solution to the problem of stable peace were to be a world federal government on the lines of the Federal government of the United States, the above consideration might well be a fatal obstacle, for it is indeed hard to conceive a true federal government which would encompass systems as diverse as we now have in the world. If, however, we can devise a model of stable peace which is somewhere short of federal government, which will involve, as it were, functional world political institutions but not in any true sense world sovereignty, then the problem looks more solvable.

There certainly seems to be no economic reason why diverse systems cannot coexist, provided that each of them is in itself workable. It seems reasonable to suppose in the light of the history of the last forty years that both Socialist and capitalist economic systems are workable, in the sense that each can produce enough internal modification of its own system to overcome its major difficulties. There is, however, no *necessity* that either of these systems be workable. We have indeed some examples of unsuccessful capitalist development, and I shall be very much surprised if in another fifty years we do not have some equally spectacular examples of unsuccessful Socialist development. It is possible for any society, no matter what its constitution and economic system, to fail to solve its internal problems. But to my mind, the ability to solve internal problems is not closely correlated with the division into Socialist and capitalist societies. Neither socialism nor capitalism are in themselves solutions to the economic problem. They merely represent different sets of conditions within which the problem must be solved. My personal preference is, of course, for a capitalist society—that is, a free-market economy which is capable of solving its problems. However, I would prefer a Socialist society that can solve its problems to a capitalist society that cannot. The whole argument between socialism and capitalism strikes me, therefore, as having a certain nineteenth-century flavor which is not necessarily relevant to the real problem of the twentieth century. Thus, the problems of coexistence of capitalism and socialism seem to me no more intrinsically difficult than the problem, say, of the coexistence of Protestantism and Catholicism. The solution to the problem of the organization of religion in society has been achieved, not by the conquest by one of these forms of religious life and organization by the other, but by the creation of a social milieu in which the threat of each to the other was removed, or at least diminished to the point where it no longer caused violence.

The problem of the impact of the economy on the institutions of warlessness then resolves itself into a number of subproblems. The first of these is, of course, how to reduce the actual strains, which differential growth or internal failure, for instance, will create in the world economy. The second problem is how to reduce the perception of these strains on the institutions of warlessness. The third problem is the problem of strength of the institutions of warlessness—that is, their ability to withstand the strains which are placed on them. Men go to war because literally they see no alternative. The development of the institutions of warlessness, therefore, must work upon two lines of approach: to make the alternative of war less favorable, and to make other alternatives more favorable. In the former category, we put such things as world law, world government, and world courts; in the latter category, we must put such things as the spread of knowledge of other alternatives than war to threat situations. This is something that is often overlooked, especially by those whose attention is concentrated, quite legitimately one may add, on the institutions of law. The better these alternatives, however, and the more vividly they are perceived, the less the problem which law has to solve. There is clearly some level of inability to solve economic problems at which violence becomes almost inevitable. It is by no means clear that the world at present is below this threshold, and it is consequently of the utmost importance to raise the level of economic knowledge and economic literacy to the point where nonviolent solutions to economic problems are clearly seen to be preferable to attempts at violent solutions.

# VII

## The economic opportunities
## following disarmament

BY HUBERT H. HUMPHREY

United States Senator from Minnesota and
Chairman of the Subcommittee on Disarmament,
Senate Foreign Relations Committee

What economic opportunities will face the United States, the
Soviet Union, and other countries once we achieve a world where
armaments no longer are being produced and maintained? The
economic questions involved relate to the transition to a peacetime economy as well as to the maintenance of a productive
economy and a high level of economic growth and employment,
once disarmament has been achieved.

Most businesses which have inquired into conversion from
defense work to reliance on nondefense income prefer conversion at a slow or moderate rate. In their view, such a pace
would result in the least disruption of business activity. Yet, this
runs head-on into the first problem: disarmament, once started,
needs to move at a relatively fast pace. The pace need not be so
fast as that of the post-World War II demobilization, which took
place within a period of about one year. At the very least, however, disarmament should proceed with all deliberate speed.

The Soviet Union proposes general and complete disarmament in five years, whereas under the United States plan, 65
per cent of a nation's military force would be dismantled in six
years with the remainder being reduced within some agreed-
upon period. Arms production would cease much sooner, and
both the United States and the Soviet Union contemplate an al-

most complete halt in the output of major armaments within about the first year of a disarmament program.

This means that major emphasis must be placed on planning, so that employment and productive capacity do not shrink suddenly to the overall detriment of the economy. *The more planning that can be done now by industry, labor, government, and local communities, the smoother the conversion would be.* Much can be accomplished by each of these four groups engaging in serious, concentrated preparatory work.

Industry—and by this I mean particularly the major defense contractors—needs to start thinking now about shifting from one form of production or defense activity to other, equally remunerative, activities. For many companies such a shift will tax the ingenuity of their planners, financial consultants, and market analysis. Since only a few companies receive the bulk of defense money (about two dozen companies account for about 70 per cent of the total), these firms have a special responsibility to plan for the conversion of their plants to meet peacetime demand.

Several of these companies might assign talent from their marketing and economic planning divisions to report on the selling opportunities which would open up at home and abroad. Disarmament would be anything but an economic depressant; rather, it should stimulate the world-wide demand for goods and services. Given the prospects for expanded trade both at home and abroad, the total planning and marketing talent of key parts of the American defense as well as nondefense industry ought to convince American businessmen, as well as American business as such, that it can make the most of a disarmed world.

The key companies have a responsibility not only to their own employees and stockholders but also to the communities in which they operate. The way in which they proceed will affect their suppliers—the many companies which sell them raw materials and parts and the numerous subcontractors whose economic future, at least in the short term, may also be tied closely to the well-being of the larger corporations.

Some of the very large companies engaged in defense business have no commercial base whatsoever. They were created as a result of defense demand. Never, or rarely, have they attempted to gear their sales activities to nonmilitary customers. Many small firms, particularly those in the fields of electronics and research and development, also have no previous experience in the commercial market. Such companies, especially the larger ones, may have more difficulty in adjusting to a peacetime economy than would those defense contractors who are primarily commercially oriented, even though the latter may receive a huge portion of their income from Pentagon orders.

The "pure" defense-type contractors, as well as the others engaged in defense business, should not be expected to make adjustments without assistance from the Federal government.

The amount of money earned by private business for defense procurement and research and development exceeds $25 billion annually. The number of workers involved in such work is somewhere between 1.5 and 2 million. These figures do not include the many workers who also are defense workers in the sense that they produce supplies, materials, and parts for the prime contractors or the first tier of defense subcontractors. Nor do they cover people working in communities which provide services to defense employees. Another group of employees includes those engaged in military construction and those who are actually members of the armed forces and their civilian counterparts.

Let us not forget that even if the disarmament plans of the United States and Soviet Russia were implemented now, not all of the $25 billion currently expended for procurement and research and development would be cut off. For example, each year the annual sum devoted to such matters as improved communications increases. In 1962, 26 per cent of the major defense and weapons programs had nothing to do with weapons *per se,* but rather were concerned with improved communications, surveillance, and to some extent with transportation. Furthermore, a good deal of research and development would not be prohibited by the terms of a treaty. As a practical matter, however, such activity would almost certainly diminish, if not disappear altogether, as a consequence of world disarmament.

Switching research and development funds from defense to peacetime projects is increasingly recognized as a key to improvement of the economic growth rate. Today over 50 per cent of all research and development in the United States is for military purposes. This has inhibited economic growth because we are not utilizing enough of our great inventiveness for productive ends. An economy that is not moving forward in the fields of research and development is a stagnant economy at best. Thus, research and development should be switched from the military to the nonmilitary track as soon as considerations of national security permit.

Before proceeding further in the discussion, the bogey of Federal intervention in the American free-enterprise system has to be faced and stared down. There is surely no argument about the fact that the defense industry as such depends for its very existence on a continuing flow of government contracts. With almost every contract, comes a degree of government "intervention"—e.g., in the form of security regulations, quality specifications, performance reviews, and the like. By the same token, the Federal government has an important role to play in effective industry conversion to a low level of defense activity.

First, the government can give industry prompt and full information about the progress of disarmament. Let us assume, for example, that a major disarmament agreement were to get under way on July 1, 1964, and that all production of armaments were to stop no later than June 30, 1965—in other words, within a year. To carry out such activity with the least risk of serious economic disruption, a schedule would have to be worked out with each company and each plant governing the cessation of particular items of defense production and spelling out the additional activity to be undertaken by the plant so as to utilize its employees and other resources. If a particular plant were to be closed down, the workers would obviously have to have alternative employment opportunities—either with their original employer or elsewhere. One cannot put a trained work force out on the streets. It is inconceivable that the Federal government, which placed the defense business in the hands of a given plant or company in the first place, would wash its hands of the consequences of withdrawing that business.

Not only must the Federal government work with the company and particular plant, but also with the appropriate union representatives, the employees of that company, the local community officials and organizations, and to some extent with state officials as well. All such activity would have one central aim: that of keeping production and employment at a level consonant with a minimum of economic dislocation to the community as well as to the particular plant.

To accomplish the ends described above, there must be a mechanism within the Federal government to deal with or to plan for individual cases. No such mechanism now exists, and because none exists, few in industry have thought the time propitious to initiate programs and plans for conversion. Within the Federal government the responsibility rests principally with four Federal agencies—the Departments of Defense, Labor, and Commerce, and the Arms Control and Disarmament Agency. Together, these four agencies have the information and the experience to plan ahead for disarmament. That they have not yet done so is an indication of the bleak prospects at the moment for a treaty on general and complete disarmament. Yet, in this area, as in many others, one thing can lead to another. Just as intense study and research on any topic may open up new possibilities for success, so concentration on the problems of conversion from defense to nondefense business may open up new avenues of progress in the disarmament negotiations themselves. If the "known" of an arms race is to be replaced by the "unknown" of a world at peace, then an essential ingredient in reducing the fear of the unknown is to pinpoint the conversion requirements of individual plants.

But the ills of individual defense plants cannot be treated in a vacuum. The nuts and bolts of any system have to be adjusted in relation to each other and to all other movable or immovable parts. This, of course, indicates another area where the Federal government must "intervene," if that is the word, to ensure maximum economic health during a period of conversion. The appropriate Federal agencies must explore the total needs of the United States economy so that individual companies or a particular industrial group can best utilize such information to plan their own conversion and expansion into the civilian sector.

I recall that back in 1953, when a settlement of the Korean conflict appeared imminent, the Department of Commerce published a useful study called "Markets After the Defense Expansion." The study surveyed the needs of each of the major segments of the economy: housing, schools, highways, chemicals, aircraft, and so forth. Forecasting, of course, is both difficult and hazardous, but the Commerce study gave business executives a better idea of what was ahead for American industry. Equally important, perhaps, it indicated that there was plenty of room for expansion of civilian production. Thus it had a psychological impact which transcended the cold message of statistical data. As we all know, the decisions of the chairman of the board can never be made by computers alone. Psychological attitudes can be, and usually are, determining factors in the success or failure of any business venture. For this reason, if for no other, the psychological aspects of conversion to peace must not be underestimated.

There is no reason why any study of future needs should be limited to the United States. Ours is not the only country in which defense spending and activity consume an enormous slice of productive capacity and national income. In considering the conversion of economic resources, therefore, the economic priorities and resources of other countries by no means should be neglected. There is unquestionably a potential market, indeed a crying economic need, for industrial expansion in every corner of the globe. I would wager that there are enough surveys, especially of the economic needs of Asia, Latin America, the Middle East, and Africa—all of them regions in early stages of industrial and agricultural development—to be distributed free to every man, woman, and child on earth. What is needed now is an examination of ways in which resources released by a cutback in defense spending can be exploited *quickly* to help meet economic requirements both at home and abroad. Let me illustrate by mentioning one very large project which could have a tremendous impact on the world's economic growth and well-being. The *sine qua non* for success of such a project, however, is effective participation by the United States government, certain international agencies, and the governments and industries of other nations. I am speaking—and let me emphasize that it is just one example out of many—of the need to harness for human benefit the unutilized or misused water resources with which our planet is blessed.

In the United States alone, there is not a single state that does not have a water problem. The problems vary, but they can be grouped under these headings: pollution abatement, water storage capacity, navigation, flood control, watershed improvement programs, irrigation needs, fish and wildlife conservation, recreation, municipal water supply, industrial water supplies, and hydroelectric power. The Business and Defense Services Administration of the Department of Commerce recently estimated that between 1958 and 1980 a total of $228 billion will have to be invested in order to solve or ameliorate the nation's water-resource problems.

What do United States water problems have to do with the economic impact of disarmament or arms-control agreements? The main connection, as I see it, is first, that both problems affect a broad stratum of our population and, second, that a solution of one of our gravest natural-resource difficulties might very well flow from a cessation of the arms race.

Is this just another utopian scheme depending upon brotherly love for its fulfillment? Not if certain essential elements can work together to diagnose and solve individual cases—in this instance, each individual water problem. These elements would consist, first, of industrial groups which are in a position to tackle the problem with drawing board and bulldozer, and second, of the organizational and financial resources of government and the community which are necessary to complete the project. For example, the Department of the Interior and the Army Corps of Engineers can delineate water needs; the Defense Department and the Arms Control and Disarmament Agency will know that "X" billions of dollars will be released as a result of a disarmament agreement; and American industry will know that a certain number of plants in a given locality will have a certain number of employees with a certain distribution of skills which a disarmament agreement would make available for alternative activity. The fusing of these three groups—government, industry, and community—ought to make for one successful and constructive program of conversion. The main question would appear to be one of organization and planning.

The press is full of actual or potential conflicts spawned by the immense problems of water on a world-wide scale. These not only impede the economic development of nations; they also cause serious political disputes leading in some cases to the threat of war. Think of a few of the great river systems in the world which run through more than one country or form a boundary between nations: the Indus River and its effect on Indo-Pakistan relations; the Jordan River system flowing through Israel, Jordan, Syria, and Lebanon; the Amazon River with its special significance for Brazil, Colombia, and Peru; the Danube River, which historically has influenced the development and mutual relations of the countries of Central and Eastern Europe; the Nile, which is a source of life not only to the United Arab Republic but also to the Sudan. These are some of the major rivers of the world which, if controlled and properly regulated, could enhance many times over the economic well-being of millions upon millions of people. Furthermore, an amicable settlement of the conflicts rising out of these major river systems might well promote better political relations among the countries immediately involved.

In the absence of any coordinated effort to solve regional water problems, each country is attempting to work out its own solution, using its own limited funds, and talents. In some cases, progress is inconceivable without prior solution of the political difficulties related to the geography of the area. In only a few cases are United States and international development programs providing assistance. Would it not help to keep a disarmed world at peace if at least some of the economic resources released by arms reduction were diverted to the establishment of an international water-development authority? Such an international institution, by utilizing the plants, employees, funds, and genius formerly devoted to arms production and the defense industry in general, could help us to make a giant stride forward in the direction of international economic development and international political stability.

For this purpose, it would not be necessary to establish just one central international water-development authority. Indeed, the most efficient arrangement would doubtless be the creation of regional authorities. The prime requirement, however, would be the formation of a pool of experience and skills for use in different projects the world over. Any such development along these lines could speed progress and improve efficiency.

Let us bear in mind that in Wagner's *Ring* cycle, the gold of the Nibelungen finally returns to the bottom of the Rhine after bringing untold misery to all who competed for sole possession of it. Our task today is to avoid analogous tragedies in the handling of our water riches. We can accomplish this task—or at least go far toward accomplishing it—by exploiting this wealth for the good of the greatest number. One of the means closest at hand is the vast socio-industrial complex hitherto devoted to the production and maintenance of defense establishments throughout the world.

The solution of local, national, regional, and international water problems is only one of several possible beneficiaries of a major disarmament agreement. There are plenty of domestic and international projects which could absorb excess productive capacity—speaking in terms of human beings as well as of plant and capital. At home, we have fantastic problems of mass transit and slum clearance. And, of course, there is always the exploration of outer space which seems insatiable in its demands for funds, talent, and resources. It would be a serious mistake, however, to look upon space exploration as an automatic substitute for our present expenditures on defense. Space is important, but our needs on this planet cry out so loudly for attention that it would be a coldhearted country indeed which gave excessive priority to the space race.

The areas are legion where reductions in military expenditures could have a decisive impact on the domestic economy as well as on economic conditions abroad. Of course, as President Kennedy indicated in response to calls for drastic reductions in the nation's space program, there is no guarantee that the money saved by a cutback will automatically be reinvested in a productive economic or social activity. But in my experience, there is sufficient enlightened self-interest on the part of our political leaders to justify the assumption that a determined effort will be made under conditions of disarmament to absorb the 10 per cent of our gross national product currently being spent on military needs. Heading the list of the areas where such funds would be most usefully spent are: education, urban renewal, urban transit, public health, the relief of economically depressed areas, the conservation of natural resources, and the overall improvement of our human environment through a variety of research and development projects.

One student of our domestic problems estimates that over and above our expenditures in the current year, the nation could invest some $5.5 to $9.5 billion in education, $10 to $15 billion in urban renewal, $4.0 billion in conservation and soil renewal, $0.5 billion in urban transit, and $1.5 billion in public health.[1] The same authority conservatively estimates that approximately 38 million Americans (more than one in every five) live in poverty. According to his analysis of this figure, which is based on 1960 statistics:

> . . . Far more than a fourth were in cousumer units (families and individuals) where the head was not employed. Far more than half were in units whose head had eight years of education or less; and almost a third were in units whose head was female. About a fourth of the total number of people living in poverty had consumer unit heads aged 65 or over. More than a fifth were nonwhite. More than a sixth were farm people. More than two fifths lived in the South.[2]

Professor Ullman concludes, and I see no reason to quarrel with his logic, that "about 20 per cent of the American domestic market remains to be developed by improving the productiveness of 38 million Americans, and thereby boosting their purchasing power."

[1] John E. Ullman, "Civilian Markets for U.S. Military Industry," *A Strategy for American Security: An Alternative to the 1964 Military Budget,* ed. Professor Seymour Melman, Columbia University (New York: April 30, 1963), pp. 16–18.

[2] "A Neglected Home Market—38 Million Americans in Poverty," *ibid.* p. 18.

These figures alone should provide incentive for timely conversion planning by government in consultation with private management. Added to this picture, however, are some very disturbing trends in our industrial economy itself.

In the first place, there is evidence that our present emphasis on military production actually tends to make United States industry "noncompetitive not only in the world market, but even within the United States." [3] We are, for instance, steadily losing ground as one of the world's leading, most efficient, and most inventive producers of machine tools. Forty per cent of the typewriters sold in the United States are of foreign manufacture. Far from pushing automation for all it is worth, American management is actually too slow to invest in the research and new equipment that would raise labor productivity and eventually provide employment for millions. In 1962, a McGraw-Hill Book Company survey reported that 60 per cent of the productive facilities in the United States were bought before 1960. Even more significant, a large proportion of the newly designed equipment now in use or on order is destined for military consumption and thus has little or no productive use.

Last August, in hearings before my subcommittee of the Senate Select Committee on Small Business, I noted that about 65 per cent of all United States research and development is paid for by the Federal government. In Germany and Japan, countries whose economies are growing by leaps and bounds and which are producing some of the most modern and efficient civilian goods, 85 cents out of every research dollar goes into the consumer market. I still have not heard a satisfactory answer to the extemporaneous question which I asked last summer at the above-mentioned hearings on "The Impact of Defense Spending in Labor Surplus Areas":

What is happening to our civilian economy as we plow more and more of our scientific personnel, our brains, into the military and into space and into atomic energy for military purposes? Where are we going to end up in this

[3] Seymour Melman, "Military Emphasis Blamed for State of Economy," *ibid.,* p. 5.

trade competition with these Belgians and Dutch, who are clever, and . . . who are spending more money for civilian aspects and will develop products cheaper, better, and more serviceable?

The international situation compels us to maintain our current level of defense spending. No one, however, should look with equanimity on the chilling effect of the arms race, which forces us to produce in massive quantities for nonproductive ends. We can derive no comfort from the fact that the talents of over half of our scientists and engineers are being tapped for military instead of exclusively civilian purposes. In a disarmed world, this serious economic imbalance can and must be corrected. The United States can and must resume its place as a model of the self-sustaining industrial society.

Some may object that the emphasis of this chapter thus far has been on programs that would require sponsorship by the Federal government or by international institutions. This is true, and we must face the fact that neither the solution of major needs nor the conversion of a $50 billion defense program to nondefense programs can be accomplished without the involvement at the ground floor of centralized government and international institutions. The largest single economic activity in the country today is the defense program which is initiated and sustained by the United States government. No responsible person would advocate taking this huge sum and abandoning it to the vicissitudes of a heterogeneous and fickle marketplace. This by no means signifies that continued large-scale participation of government in the economy cancels out the need for gradual and even increasing *private* participation in the mapping out of economic conversion programs. Ours is, after all, a free-enterprise economy, and no responsible official would be so unscrupulous as to use the conversion of the defense industry as a foot in the door for outright state ownership of the means of production. The problem cannot be stated in these terms. The only realistic way is to recognize, as large segments of private industry have already recognized, that only government and international programs of considerable magnitude can absorb most of the sums that are currently expended on defense.

As stated earlier, many of the key companies receiving the bulk of defense orders have had little or no experience with the commercial marketplace. In 1959 (the last year for which figures are available), some fifteen companies received over $10 billion from defense contracts. These fifteen companies are completely defense-oriented. Right now they ought to be working with the government to determine how the skills of their employees and their plant equipment might be utilized to enhance their future economic prosperity. Obviously, they cannot receive a monopoly on any project. But given the responsibility of the government to maintain full employment, and given the burden of unemployment already weighing down the United States economy, these defense-oriented companies must turn not only toward the marketplace, but *rather must first attempt to cooperate and coordinate their adjustment activities* with government. This is the only visible way to solve those national and international economic and social problems which will help to keep a disarmed world disarmed and at peace.

# VIII

## Disarmament and the population problem

BY GRENVILLE CLARK

Lawyer, author, with Louis B. Sohn,
of *World Peace through World Law*

I shall undertake to show that, while the prevention of undue population growth is probably impossible until disarmament is achieved, the release, through complete disarmament, of vast resources to raise living standards in the "have-not" areas of the world could bring about effective population control within a few decades.

For the purposes of this chapter, I ask the reader to accept several assumptions: (1) that total national disarmament and the establishment of the world institutions necessary thereto will have been achieved by the end of 1982; (2) that during the twenty years, 1963–82, the world population of about 3.1 billion will increase to about 4.4 billion; (3) that of this estimated 1982 population nearly 60 per cent or about 2.06 billion persons will be living in dire poverty; and (4) that by 1982 there will have been established a world development authority and a reliable world revenue system whereby some $60 billion per annum will be available to alleviate the economic condition of the most impoverished areas of the world. These assumptions are, I believe, soundly based upon a careful appraisal of probable developments in the next twenty years.

For such an appraisal, one should first consider the seventeen-year period, 1946–62, after World War II—a period often regarded as one of utter failure and frustration because of the many protracted and sterile efforts for disarmament. But while the failures and frustrations cannot be denied, these years should also be regarded as a period of necessary adjustment and gestation during which the people of the world began to understand that world order will require not only disarmament, but also the same kind of legislative, executive, and judicial institutions on a world scale as experience has shown to be necessary for the maintenance of internal order in local communities and within nations.

Reflecting this gradual enlightenment, the year 1961 included the March 17 statement of all the Prime Ministers of the British Commonwealth calling for "total world-wide disarmament" and for a "substantial and adequately armed" world police force; the McCloy-Zorin agreement of September 20, whereby the objective of "general and complete" disarmament was unequivocally accepted by the two superpowers; and President Kennedy's United Nations speech of September 25 in which he summoned the world to a "peace race" based upon total national disarmament.

Despite this progress and the convening of the seventeen-nation disarmament conference in March, 1962, I can see little likelihood of any comprehensive disarmament agreement in the near future. It seems clear that the mutual suspicions of East and West will remain too deep and their positions too far apart to justify the hope that the principal powers will actually reach an agreement for total disarmament within the period ending in 1965.

On the other hand, the chances for the making and ratification of such an agreement toward the end of the ensuing seven-year period, 1966–72, would seem to be more than even, for the reason that several important influences for genuine peace are likely to converge at that time, and together constitute a force sufficient to sweep aside the formidable obstacles which have theretofore blocked the way.

Paramount among these influences will be, I judge, a steadily mounting concern relative to the consequences of nuclear war. We must remember that until a disarmament agreement comes into actual operation, both the risks and the inexorable demands of the arms race will certainly continue and may even increase.

As predicted by Secretary of State Rusk in March 1962, the already vast nuclear power of the two sides will probably double by the end of 1965. In the absence of a disarmament agreement, this destructive power would presumably double again within a few years thereafter, while at the same time armament costs would probably increase still further. In these circumstances, is it not reasonable to suppose that the pressure on all government to stop the arms race will almost certainly intensify from year to year? Simultaneously, through expanded public education and discussion, there should develop a far better-informed public opinion in many nations with respect to the kind of world organization required for the achievement and maintenance of disarmament; and, beyond this, there should develop a wider understanding of the truth that the elimination of national armaments is indispensable to a solution of the population problem. It is through this combination of greater concern with a better comprehension of the remedy that we may reasonably expect the long-sought-for disarmament agreement—not at some indefinitely remote date, but by the end of 1972.

Such an agreement having once been reached and ratified, the process of actual disarmament should require no more than ten years, in which case the goal of a disarmed world subject to enforceable world law in the limited field of war prevention would be realized by the end of 1982.

During this twenty-year period through 1982, it is safe to predict that the population problem will become steadily more acute. This seems inevitable, when we consider two determining factors: (1) that as of 1962, the rate of population growth in the poverty-stricken regions of the world exceeded 2 per cent per annum; and (2) that so long as large expenditures on armaments continue, it will be impracticable to furnish economic aid to these "have-not" areas on a scale sufficient to bring about any important improvement in their living standards and thus to provide the environment and motivation for any substantial reduction in population growth.

It should always be remembered that the population problem is almost entirely concentrated in the poorest areas of the world. Various large countries (including the United States, Canada, and Australia) could doubtless maintain at a good standard of living populations even four times as large as those of 1962; whereas even a doubling to 900 million of the population of India or to 1,300 million of that of China might well cancel out the benefits of outside aid even on a massive scale. Accordingly, the real problem is not to prevent even a considerable population increase of the world as a whole, but rather to hold to a minimum any increases in areas which are already poverty-stricken.

It may be suggested that the development of inexpensive contraceptive pills or other simple means of family limitation will alone suffice to solve this problem. Unfortunately, however, any such hope leaves out of account the all-important factor of motivation for the use of such remedies. The estimated 2.6 billion impoverished and largely illiterate people who in 1982 will probably still have an average annual per capita income of less than $100, would have little incentive to make use of even the simplest and cheapest birth-control techniques. For experience shows that even when the means for family limitation are readily available, they are not fully adopted by people living in extreme poverty, who can see no hope for any real improvement in the lot of themselves and their descendants. It seems clear, therefore, that, along with new and inexpensive techniques for birth control, a drastic improvement in the living standards of the impoverished areas is necessary—*both* being indispensable for any substantial reduction in population growth.

Assuming, then, that a great improvement in the standards of living of the poorer nations is essential for population control, the next thing to realize is that the flow of aid from the industrialized nations is now on a scale utterly inadequate to the end in view.

A liberal estimate of total economic aid in 1962 to all the low-income areas of the world is $10 billion from all sources—governmental, United Nations, and private—or about $9 billion if we choose to omit aid to China from the Soviet bloc of, say, $1 billion. Assuming that the 1962 population of all the low-income areas is about 1.8 billion persons, the estimated total aid of $10 billion would provide less than $6 per capita; while if China, with nearly 700 million people is excluded, the estimated $9 billion in aid of about 1.1 billion persons would provide about $8 per capita.

Taking India as a concrete example, total outside aid in 1962 may be estimated at $2.2 billion which, when applied to India's population of 450 million, is equal to about $5 per capita, or $25 per annum for a family of five.

Can anyone reasonably suppose that aid on this restricted scale—whether $5, $6 or, $8 per capita per annum—can be effective to bring about the drastic improvement in living standards necessary to alleviate the vast disparities between the "have" and "have-not" peoples of the world and to furnish sufficient motivation for adequate population control?

Accordingly, it seems apparent that, however valuable present efforts may be as a manifestation of good will and as a means of gaining experience, the scale must be radically increased in order to accomplish only what is barely necessary to make any real impression on the living standards of most of the countries involved.

In contrast to the estimated total aid of only $10 billion in 1962, the $60 billion per annum program which is assumed for the period after total disarmament may seem very large. But a brief consideration will, I believe, show that this amount will be little enough to meet the need.

Let it be remembered that this task calls for a radical and reasonably fast improvement of the living standards of no less than 2.6 billion persons presumed to be living in 1982 under conditions of dire poverty. Thus the assumed $60 billion in annual aid is seen to amount to only $23 per capita to cover the immense programs in education, transportation, industralization, agriculture, housing, health, and so forth which could alone suffice to have any real effect upon living standards within a reasonable time.

By contrast, it should be recalled that the remarkable results achieved in Israel during the 1948–62 period have been aided by an inflow of outside capital equal to at least $100 per capita per annum, or more than four times as much per capita as would be available after 1982 from an annual inflow of $60 billion to all the low-income areas.

And finally, let it be emphasized that this program would only take effect after the burden of national armaments had been entirely lifted, in an amount which in 1962 already comes to $120 billion and will probably increase to $140 billion per annum by the time a disarmament agreement actually comes into force. Accordingly, the new program would involve no additional tax burden. On the contrary, even assuming that as much as $15 billion per annum would be needed for the world police force and the various functions of the world organization other than the $60 billion for aid to the low-income areas, the total new expenditure would come to no more than $75 billion per annum or $45–$65 billion *less* than the armaments costs from which the nations would have been relieved.

As applied to the United States, the saving would be perhaps $30 billion per annum resulting from the elimination of a prospective annual armaments cost of $60 billion partially offset by, say, $3 billion for internal police forces and, say, $27 billion as our share of the assumed $75 billion annual budget of the world organization. It might or might not be that this saving of $30 billion per annum would be reflected in a reduction of taxation; but, in any event, it would represent a true saving in that this amount would be released either for tax reduction or for badly needed internal uses.

The conclusions to be drawn from the foregoing review, therefore, are: first, that $60 billion per annum for aid to the world's impoverished areas will be no more than the minimum needed to achieve the rise in living standards which is indispensable to any important reductions in population growth; and second, that, having in mind the immense savings from total national disarmament, this expense can be borne without difficult by the industrialized nations.

I turn now to the problem of what could be accomplished *after* the coming into force of an agreement for general and complete disarmament, asking the question: Assuming an agreement for general and complete disarmament by the end of 1972, the completion of the disarmament process by the end of 1982 and then a large and sustained program of economic aid to the poorest nations of the world, what could reasonably be expected during the sixty years thereafter by way of population control?

It should be emphasized that the first decade following the coming into force of the disarmament agreement would necessarily be a period mainly of planning and preparation. During these ten years, 1973–1982, the new institutions of the world organization would be set up; and after the year or two required for this purpose, there would follow the agreed-upon process of total disarmament by each and every nation resulting by the end of 1982 in a disarmed world, save only for a strong world police force and certain internal police forces strictly limited in number and very lightly armed.

Parallel with this process, the new legislative, executive, judicial and quasi-judicial agencies, including the world development authority and the world revenue system, would have commenced to function, and the work of improving the economic condition of the impoverished regions would at last be under way with machinery and resources fairly adequate to the task.

Without doubt, this first decade would also be devoted to the professional and technical training of indigenous personnel on a great scale. Such a training program would be a clear necessity in order to provide at least 3 million young men and women (only one to every 866 of the populations in need) to be teachers, doctors, engineers, architects and builders, lawyers, judges, and administrators in the low-income areas, containing the assumed 2.6 billion persons for whom aid could now begin to flow on a scale never before remotely possible. Such training would be carried out in part by sending during the assumed preparatory decade as many as 1.5 million carefully chosen young people to Western educational institutions, and also by enlarging or creating many new professional and technical schools and colleges in the various underdeveloped countries. In this way, indigenous trained personnel would be ready to administer the gradually growing funds which would become available parallel with the year-by-year reduction of national armaments.

Parallel also with actual disarmament and this training program, comprehensive planning would doubtless proceed as to the ways and means of making use of the new resources and skills so that, by the time the disarmament process was completed and the assumed $60 billion per annum became available, the foundations would have been laid for well-prepared and adequately staffed programs.

During the preparatory period just mentioned, actual progress in the improvement of living standards would necessarily be rather slight, since, although diminishing year by year, a considerable burden of armament expense would still exist. For example, if we assume that the process of actual disarmament gets under way in 1973 on the basis of a 10 per cent reduction per annum in each year through 1982, the assumed armament expense of $140 billion per annum would steadily decrease, thereby making practicable the allotment of corresponding amounts for the use of the world organization. It might well be that all of this saving would not be placed at the disposal of the world organization, but it is reasonable to suppose that, say, $10 billion would be available for the world development authority during each of the first several years of actual disarmament, and that, as the process continued, these amounts would increase to $15 billion, $30 billion, and $50 billion per annum as the disarmament process drew toward its end. Thus, while the practical effect upon living standards and consequently upon population growth might be small during this first decade, the basis would have been laid for tremendous accomplishment in the period following total disarmament.

It is in this subsequent period, with the preparatory work done and with the assumed infusion into the low-income areas of $60 billion per annum, that definite and reasonably prompt progress could confidently be expected. For, although our assumed $60 billion per annum would provide outside aid of only about $23 per capita per annum, this would be supplemented by indigenous capital in accordance with the varying capacities of the various nations. In some instances this contribution would necessarily be small, but it would in all cases be a factor of some consequence, and in certain instances might amount to as much as the aid provided through the world development authority.

If, for example, we assume that the average local and national contributions amounted to $12 per capita per annum in respect of 2.6 billion people, the total annual expenditure for the great campaign of economic and social betterment would be financed by an annual expenditure of $35 per capita, or $91 billion per annum. In these circumstances, who can doubt that even in the first twenty years after the completion of the disarmament process there would be so great an improvement in the standard of living of the impoverished peoples as to effect an important alteration in their outlook upon life and, as part thereof, in their motivation in respect of family limitation?

Still better results in population control should follow in the period of, say, four decades, 2003–2042, in consequence of the combination of steadily improving living standards and the probable advances in birth-control methods which should by that time put them within reach of even the poorest people.

As a reasonable prognosis, I suggest that in this forty-year period population growth in the low-income areas could be gradually reduced to no more than 1.5 per cent per annum and world population growth to less than 1 per cent per annum. If so, the total world population in 2043 might not exceed about 8.5 billion rather than the 11.7 billion to which it would increase if, during the entire eighty years from 1963–2042, population growth continued at the 1.7 per cent rate of the 1946–62 period.

This supposition that, as a result of general and complete disarmament and massive economic aid to the most needy areas, the world population can be held to less than 9 billion as of 2043 will doubtless be thought too optimistic by some demographers. Among other objections, the fact may be cited that industrialization and rising living standards do not always, at least in the short run, bring about reduced population growth; and the rapid increases of population in Britain and Japan during their industrial revolutions may be cited. I suggest, however, that the conditions in the world's most impoverished regions are now very different in that, while Japan and Britain were not anxious in the nineteenth century to limit their populations and even welcomed increased numbers, such countries as China, India, Pakistan, and Egypt will by 1973 be almost desperately concerned to prevent further increases and will willingly cooperate to that end. If so, it seems altogether probable that the predicted results would promptly follow the assumed large inflow of aid which would be possible in a disarmed world.

To those accustomed to the 3.1 billion world population of

1962 (not to speak of those who recall the world of 1920 with only about 2 billion people), a world with a population of 8.5 billion may seem a crowded planet indeed. Yet with the aid of modern science, it need not be intolerably crowded and should, in fact, be a better world in having eliminated the worst extremes of poverty and hardship which so badly mar our boasted civilization of 1962.

In any event, the restriction of population growth within these limits is in all likelihood the best that can be done (without the unwanted help of nuclear war or widespread famine and disease); and the all-important point to be grasped is that even this degree of population control will be dependent upon the achievement of total disarmament not later than 1982.

By general consent, the two paramount problems of our time which in some way affect all the people of the world are the problem of preventing nuclear war and that of population control. It is idle to argue as to which of these problems is the more important, since the solution of both is essential to a satisfactory future for the human race.

What I have sought to demonstrate is that the two problems are closely interrelated, especially in the respect that population control is dependent upon disarmament, so as to make practicable the provision of sufficient aid from the industrialized nations to bring about so great an improvement in the living standards of the impoverished areas as to create among their people the necessary motivation for family limitation.

In other words, I conclude that, without total disarmament, population control would be impracticable and the world would have to reconcile itself to all the evils which would certainly follow from excessive and hungry populations in large portions of the globe; while, on the other hand, the realization of total disarmament would open the way to a tremendous improvement in living standards and the consequent stabilization of population within a relatively few years.

It follows that those who strive for peace and those who strive for population control should strike hands in a united effort for the preservation and welfare of mankind.

# IX

## The struggle of ideas

BY ARTHUR LARSON

A major obstacle to disarmament may be the fear that the values of one's culture might not prevail or even survive unless ultimately backed by armaments. It is difficult to judge how widespread this feeling may be, since it is not the kind of sentiment that people are apt to express openly. Nevertheless, anyone who has dealt with this problem over a period of years, officially and unofficially, and who has had experience with conferences, question periods, and debates on the subject, realizes that this is a fact which cannot be ignored.

This fear appears to be the result of two misconceptions. The first is an overestimation of the sheer ideological power of communism. The second is an underestimation of the power of the ideas associated with the Western community of nations, and the ability of these nations to achieve identification with the newly developing nations on the strength of these ideas.

The notion that communism has some sort of intrinsic vitality and attractiveness which inexorably leads to its acceptance on the strength of ideological force alone is a myth. It has no support either in history or in current events.

The best evidence of this is the fact that, with one or two minor exceptions, a Communist regime has never been installed as the result of free democratic elections.

Conversely, where Communist regimes have been installed, it has almost always been against a backdrop of force, either exercised or threatened. The pattern followed in Eastern Europe is typical. It was the overwhelming power of the Soviet Union, poised a short distance away, which formed the canopy of menace under which minorities were able to seize power in one country after another. If anyone doubts this, he need only be referred to the Hungarian Revolution, which demonstrated how swiftly this potentiality of Soviet armed force could become an actuality.

While there are different interpretations of the Soviet Union's motives in attempting to build a strong missile base in Cuba, I should like to suggest an explanation related to the East European pattern just described. In this pattern, the immensely powerful nearby outside military force acts, so to speak, as an upper millstone. The nether millstone is provided by a group of Communist (or pro-Castro) sympathizers and guerrilla fighters within the particular country. Neither of these, acting alone, could ordinarily impose a Communist regime, as we have seen from history. The imposition of such a regime from outside is too flagrant a violation of international standards to be tolerated, and runs too many risks of bringing defeat and discredit on the Soviet Union directly. Moreover, the internal group, acting alone, is usually too small to bring about the change, particularly since most people in an average country, however discontented with their lot, are not inclined to join in the most fanatical and bloody type of revolution. But now suppose that the Soviet Union had been able to emplace sufficient rockets to bring Venezuela and various other Latin American countries "under their guns." This upper millstone, acting with the local pro-Communist or pro-Castro forces, might possibly be enough to grind the country into submission. Except for the use of rockets instead of more old-fashioned armaments, this would be an almost perfect replica of the East European formula.

In the kind of disarmed and warless world here contemplated, the upper millstone would be removed. As Walter Millis has pointed out in his chapter, it would probably be unrealistic to look for the complete elimination of force applied to internal political change. So here, if local political, economic, and social forces are driving the people to revolutionary change, it would be both impossible and probably undesirable to try to rule out all resort to force—always provided that the internal turmoil does not threaten international peace by involving outside powers. If an indigenous movement is able to command sufficient internal support, without reliance on outside help, to bring about a certain change, it would be presumptuous and illegal for other countries to interfere. Indeed, the kind of change that would be brought about in this way should presumably cause no particular alarm, because by being indigenous and not dependent on a large outside Communist power, it would lack the essential component making such a change dangerous: the reduction of the smaller country to satellite status.

There is an interesting parallel here to the relation between force and fanatical revolutionary ideas in other periods, notably that of the French Revolution. Within the French Revolution, as within the Communist Revolution, there were intellectuals who were so convinced of the inherent vitality of their revolutionary doctrines that they were satisfied to let these doctrines propagate themselves by ideological vigor alone. However, in the French Revolution as in the Communist Revolution, this group lost out, and the day was carried by those revolutionaries who preferred to assist ideological force with a generous amount of armed force. Where armed force was so used, the ideas of the French Revolution were translated into action. Where such force was not used, no such direct result followed—although, of course, these ideas have gradually worked themselves out in intervening centuries.

Behind the myth of the inherent invincibility of unaided Communist ideology lies another myth: the notion that there is in fact a Communist ideology. If an ideology must be a set of ideas bearing some reasonable relation to what goes on in practice, it surely must be evident by now that there is no gleaming, unified, consistent package which can be called the Communist ideology. Certainly it is not Marxism. It has been repeatedly demonstrated that a large part of what goes on inside the Soviet Union is the exact opposite of Marxism, and the demonstration need not be repeated here. The fact is well known throughout the world, except in a few very remote places where occasional earnest but unsophisticated individuals may be temporarily taken in by invocations of Marxism. The Soviet ideologists themselves know this as well as anyone, but their standard answer is that their current non-Marxian practices are only a necessary stage along the road to Marxian communism. The trouble with this explanation is that, with every year that passes, the realities of Soviet life draw further away from Marxism rather than closer to it. Instead of approaching the ideal of "from each according to his ability, to each according to his need," every year the incentive principle is pressed more vigorously into service—a principle, of course, borrowed directly from private enterprise. Every year there is greater reliance on profits and less on decrees. Every year there is more decentralization rather than less. Every year there is increased emphasis on productivity, although it was the excessive productivity of capitalism which Marx predicted would bring about its downfall. Every year the gap between the rich and the poor seems to grow greater. The secretary of the Rayon Committee gets twenty-five times the pay of the average worker (the Secretary of State of the United States, in contrast, gets only six times the pay of an average American industrial worker). Members of the Supreme Soviet may get 40,000 rubles a year, while there are large numbers of Russian peasants and workers still getting something in the neighborhood of 400 rubles a year. The rawest drives of the piece-work mechanism, for which one must go to the worst capitalistic excesses of Marx's time to find a parallel, are enthusiastically applied in the collective farms and factories of the Soviet Union. For example, the unit of pay on a collective farm is the so-called day's work. A man can amass as many units of "day's work" as he can wring out of his own exertions and those of his family. If he wants to work all day and all night and force his children and aged grandmother to do the same, he will earn just that many more units, and eventually he may find his picture posted on the collective-farm bulletin board as a particularly meritorious worker.

We increasingly see reliance on the price system for controlling distribution and on the profit system for giving direction to the economy. For example, a certain Mr. Pavlov, who was having difficulty getting potato peelers produced, was reported as proposing this solution, by the Associated Press on February 26, 1958:

> He suggested production could be stimulated by increasing the wholesale price 3.5 per cent and rewarding factory officials and workers who would turn out more peelers.

At almost the same time, the following news report by Reuters of a Resolution of February 25, 1958 of the Central Committee of the Czechoslovak Communist party appeared in the paper:

> The Resolution said the present system of organizing and directing the economy "no longer corresponds to the needs of a rapidly expanding economy. . . ."
> Factories will be allowed to share in the profit from their own productions so as to give them a financial basis to decide independently about their own investment, general repairs, and other projects.

Thus it is that, as the pace of industrialization quickens in these countries, and as they begin to use the language of "rapidly expanding economy," they also quite naturally begin to use such words as "profit" and to talk about independent investment.

In short, if the direction of present events in the more industrialized Communist countries is extrapolated, one reaches something much closer to a typical private-enterprise economy than to the classless, profitless, propertyless paradise in which distribution is related only to need and not to ability. No Communist ideologist has yet explained how a series of events each more non-Marxian than the last can be a transition to a Marxian finale.

Most of the responsible leaders around the world are quite well aware of this gulf between Marxist theory and Soviet practice. In addition, they cannot help being increasingly aware of the violent disagreement within Communist ranks on what the true Communist gospel is. The difference between seeking the triumph of communism through peaceful coexistence and achieving it through violent and bloody warfare is no mere detail. Neither is the question whether there is one road to socialism or many, or whether Communists should "let all flowers bloom" or only one. The Soviet Union ridicules the Chinese for herding people into "communes"; the Chinese berate the Russians for their obtuseness in failing to see that this is precisely what communism is all about. The Yugoslavs settle for more or less individualized farming; other Communist countries insist on collectivizing farms. The Soviet Union itself zigzags between encouraging private production through small personal farm plots, and taking away the private plots and livestock in the name of ideology and supposed efficiency.

If, then, we picture communism as saying to the rest of the world "do as we do," this is confusing enough, but if they also add "and do as we say" the confusion becomes complete.

What is it that the Communists have to offer in the "struggle of ideas"? Actually, it is not so much Marxian ideology with Leninist amendments as a pragmatic set of experiences in hastening industrial development through state capitalism and intensive governmental involvement in the economy. What the leaders of the newer countries are interested in, being pragmatists themselves, is not so much an intellectual formulation as a workable model which has proved itself in practice. If the particular newly developing country is especially concerned with increasing agricultural production, and if it sees that both Communist China and the Soviet Union have so far made a botch of agriculture, this will probably create a greater impression than the contents of *Das Kapital* and the Communist Manifesto.

In a disarmed and warless world, then, there need be no fear that the uncommitted nations of the world will be spellbound and hynotized in some mystic way by the irresistible intellectual magic of Communist ideology. If Communist experience should at certain points develop methods that these countries find more suitable to meet specific problems, there should be no cause for alarm or surprise when some such methods are in fact emulated. This, however, leads us to the next question, which is whether we have not underestimated the intrinsic power of Western ideas and experience, and their potential for creating identification with the newer countries.

The "struggle of ideas," whether carried on under present conditions or under the hypothetical conditions of a warless world, is not a struggle between revolution and the *status quo*. It is rather a struggle between two kinds of revolution.

One of the great ideological disadvantages from which the Western community is now suffering is that it has somehow been maneuvered into the position of being antichange. This, if true, would be a hopeless position. Most of the people in the world want change, and one cannot blame them.

The people of the Western world, then, if they are to face with equanimity the struggle of ideas in a warless world, must remind themselves that they are revolutionaries and the sons of revolutionaries and that they are part of the most radical politico-economic experiment in human history—an experiment which has reached only a precarious mid-point.

Barbara Ward, in her book *Rich Nations and Poor Nations,* lists four revolutions generated by the nations of the Atlantic Community: (1) the revolution of equality, of both men and nations; (2) the revolution of expectation of material change leading to a better world here and now; (3) the biological revolution represented by a rapidly expanding population; and (4) the scientific revolution, through the application of science to all human affairs, including the economic.

She points out that countries of the North Atlantic lost touch with the Asian, African, and Latin American countries because the latter did not share in these revolutions. In other words, we would be entitled to draw from Miss Ward's analysis a conclusion precisely the opposite of the usual one: if there is a lack of understanding between the Atlantic Community and the newly developed countries, it is because the Atlantic Community has been revolutionary and most of the rest of the world has not— and not the other way around.

So far as the place of the Communist Revolution in all this is concerned, in its present manifestation it appears mostly as an attempt to move in upon these ongoing revolutions and hasten them along at forced-draft pace. At least a case could be made for this in theory, although in practice, as shown above, the story may be somewhat different.

It is therefore incumbent on the Western nations to realize, with or without a warless world, that the real revolution in the world is *their* revolution, and that it is up to them to see this revolution through and to take responsibility for its consequences all over the world.

It is the force and validity of these revolutionary ideas that count, and that will control the course of the struggle of ideas. If communism wants to claim these ideas as its own, this of itself will not make the ideas any better or worse than they already intrinsically are.

Let us look briefly at the four revolutions of our time, and see how the struggle of ideas would work itself out in respect to these revolutions.

The first is the revolution of equality of men and of nations. As to equality between individuals, this takes many forms, and in most of them it is still the Western nations that are setting the pace. As to political equality, their representative democratic systems with genuine individual voting power are certainly a higher expression of equality than control of a large country by a minority Communist party, with no real effective individual vote. As to legal equality, this also reaches its highest peak in the Western systems, where equality before the law is a fact as well as a principle, and where the individual person can call the state and state officials to account on equal terms in court in a way unthinkable in Communist countries. As to economic equality, comparison of actual standards of living, whether absolute or relative as between people of the same country, shows that the Western style of revolution is so far the most successful. As to racial economy, there is considerable room for improvement in all parts of the world. While this is the one area in which the Western nations are perhaps most vulnerable, the recent ugly racial events in Bulgaria may serve as a reminder that racism is a universal problem, and that its counterparts in religious, communal, and tribal tension are found in some form almost everywhere.

When we come to the application of the principle of equality to nations, if the nations of the West really believe what they say about their principles, and particularly if they really believe what they say about the Soviet Union, they should logically conclude that, in any struggle of ideas, they have here an enormous and perhaps decisive advantage. The Western countries stoutly maintain that they support the principle of self-determination, and the right of every nation to govern itself without outside interference. They also maintain that the actual and ultimate goal of the Soviet Union is to bring under satellite status as many nations of the world as it can, just as it has done with nations of Eastern Europe.

If they really believe that this accurately describes the position of the West and of communism, how can they possibly draw any conclusion except that all the newly independent countries must necessarily be firmly identified with the West on this point, and implacably opposed to the Communist position? We are dealing here with nations which have spent many years of painful and sometimes bloody struggle to achieve national independence. Is such a nation knowingly and voluntarily going to throw away this hard-won independence, and trade one brand of imperial rule for another? To reach such a conclusion, one would have to attribute to these countries a naïveté and an incompetence to look after their own national interests that surpasses credibility. True, there have been times when some national leaders seemed less than fully alert to this danger, and in at least one case, that of Castro, we may be witnessing an exception to the rule. Generally, the newly independent countries have been highly sensitive to possible encroachments on their national integrity, from communism or anything else. Again and again we have seen countries like Egypt, Iraq, and some of the African countries taking strict repressive measures against Communists when they appeared to be going too far in interference with internal affairs.

In short: either the Soviet Communists want to make satellites of all the new countries or they do not. If they do, they are certain to lose in the struggle of ideas. If they do not, then the stakes in the struggle are not as serious as the West has maintained.

In any event, the Western democracies, from their side, should do everything in their power to show that the principle of equality and integrity of nation-states is respected in conduct as well as in theory. There are many ways in which this can be done, of which one or two examples might be indicated. A direct application of the principle is the "one nation, one vote" rule in the General Assembly of the United Nations. Whatever attacks may be made on this principle from the point of view of abstract logic, it ought to be defended vigorously as not only the most conspicuous symbol but also one of the most practical applications of the principle of equality of nations. Similarly, in everyday dealings with the smaller and newer countries, every precaution should be taken to avoid instances of undue domination or unseemly paternalism. For example, when Tunisia had become an independent country, for a time France tried to insist that other countries must conduct their foreign relations with Tunisia through France. As to the United States, there have been times when in spite of its admittedly deep interest in certain strategic countries of the world, it seems to have overstepped proper bounds in publicly attempting to influence the internal affairs of such countries.

As to the "revolution of equality," then, whether of individuals or of nations, in a struggle of ideas in a warless world, the advantage could lie strongly with the original proprietors of the revolution around the Atlantic Community.

A second modern revolution is that produced by the conviction that man can materially improve his lot and create a better world by his own efforts. This stands in contrast to various philosophies which put stress rather on rewards in a life to come, or on the virtues of self-abnegation, or on the monotonous unending cycle of life with no progress or upward movement.

In translating this idea into material goods, the key word has been "productivity." One cannot refrain here from pointing out that the concept of productivity as the key to the economic problem, which we take so easily for granted, and which Chairman Khrushchev has espoused with such emphasis, is basically a Western idea, which has rather belatedly been taken over by communism. Chairman Khrushchev is now challenging other nations to races in productivity. But if Marx were alive today, he would probably bet on capitalism in any productivity race. In the opening pages of the Communist Manifesto, we find such a passage as this:

> The bourgeoisie, during its rule of scarce 100 years, has created more massive and more colossal productive forces than have all preceding generations together.

Indeed, it is all too easily forgotten today, by Communists and non-Communists alike, that Marx's entire theory of the downfall of capitalism was based on the idea that there would be too much productivity. Thus, he wrote in the same work:

> Modern bourgeois society, with its relations of production, of exchange and of property, a society that has conjured up such gigantic means of production and of exchange, is like a sorcerer, who is no longer able to control the powers of the nether world whom he has called up by his spells . . . and why? Because there is too much civilization, too much means of subsistence, too much industry, too much commerce.

One often wonders how the Communists explain this text to the people of the newly developing countries, who would undoubtedly be glad to take their chances with "too much means of subsistence, too much industry, too much commerce."

In addition to productivity, the principle most relevant to the revolution of material change leading to a better world is that of the proper relation of government to the economy and to people. It is at this point that the contrast between the private-enterprise democracies, on the one hand, and the Communist or Socialist countries, on the other, has been thought to be most conspicuous. Superficially, the pattern might seem to look like this: the private-enterprise democracies claim to believe in minimal government involvement in the economy; communism avowedly favors heavy government involvement in the economy; the newly developing countries almost invariably find that heavy governmental involvement in the economy is necessary; therefore—so the conclusion supposedly runs—the newly developing economies should find communism more closely suited to their needs than private enterprise.

There are two principal flaws in this formulation.

The first is that the central principle of the relation of government to business and to people in the Western countries is not this kind of classical laissez-faire. Rather, it is best summed up in a quotation from Abraham Lincoln, which has now become one of his best-known sayings: "The proper role of government is to do for people what needs to be done, but what they cannot of themselves do at all or do so well." Applying this principle to the newly developing countries, one finds, first, that there is more that needs to be done for people, and second, that a larger proportion of it has to be done by the government; but the principle itself is valid, although the facts are different.

If there is misunderstanding on the part of the newer countries about the ideology of the Western countries, this is largely the fault of the Western countries themselves. All too often they have pictured their system as one of absolutely free private enterprise, with a government strictly keeping hands off, except in highly unusual circumstances. This has been particularly true of some people in the United States. Consequently, we have seen the spectacle of Americans (the public sector of whose economy is 20 per cent) objecting to the giving of economic aid to "those Socialists" in India (whose public sector is 5 per cent). Although the Indians like to call themselves Socialists and the Americans to call themselves private enterprisers, actually the American economy contains quantitatively four times as great a "socialized" component as the Indian.

Even within the American economy, Americans persist in clinging to outmoded fictions about the relative independence of parts of the economy. They still love to think of the American farmer as a great rugged individualist, dependent on no other person, and least of all the government, whereas in fact the government is deeply involved in his prices, his acreages, his choice of crops, his seeds, his pesticides, his fertilizers, his product research, and almost every detail of his operation. Is this the picture that the farmer of "Socialist" India has of the capitalist farmer in America? Probably not. Why should it be? It is not even the picture that Americans have, although the facts are directly before them.

The Lincoln formula has proved to be amazingly adaptable and successful in practice. Of course, as a principle to be tested on a global basis, it obviously leaves a great deal of elbow room for judging when the government can do something better than people can do it privately. But as a practical working principle, it has obvious superiority over classical socialism, which demands that the instruments of production be put in the hands of the government whether the government can do the job better or not. Socialism requires acceptance of the completely unproved proposition, which must be accepted as a doctrinaire act of faith, that government is necessarily more efficient and more equitable a producer and distributor of goods than private enterprise in all instances.

This brings us to the second point about the relation of government to business and people, which is this: It is now becoming apparent that governmental control, planning, and operation by decree is an inefficient way of running a highly developed industrial economy.

It used to be thought, particularly during the time of the Great Depression and for some time after, that the movement toward socialism was a steady upward line which inexorably would carry all of the industrial nations of the world to more and more nationalization, until complete socialism appeared at the end of the process. This view had some support in the observed facts of the time, although there was a failure to realize that the special conditions of the Depression followed by a period of total war made for an artificial amount of government involvement in business. Moreover, particularly in the United States, the persistence of laissez-faire thought had resulted in an abnormally low degree of government contact with business prior to that time. There was thus some ground to be made up before even a balanced relation between the governmental and the private was struck. However, those that believed that this rising line of centralization and nationalization could be projected indefinitely into the future were due for a surprise after World War II.

At that time, the British began to pursue a policy of nationalizing some major industries, but economic problems persisted. At the same time, countries like West Germany and Japan, pursuing essentially private-enterprise methods, achieved a much faster rate of growth. Whether because of this observation, or for other political and economic reasons, Britain not only halted but even attempted to reverse the trend in nationalization.

Perhaps the most eloquent evidence of the change of direction is a poll taken by Elmo C. Wilson and published in his bulletin of February, 1958. Of the people of eighteen industrialized nations of the free world, only about 8 per cent said that they were in favor of the government's taking over the ownership and management of large industries. The rest said that the government ought to leave them alone or, at most, regulate them but not try to manage them. Among these countries were a number that are sometimes loosely referred to as "Socialist," such as the Scandinavian countries and Australia. Indeed, in these countries the percentages were the lowest of all. Moreover, even the Socialist parties of such industrial countries as Germany and Great Britain have officially renounced state ownership of industry as policy.

We may now put two observed facts side by side: One, that the newly developing countries almost invariably find a high degree of government participation in industrial development necessary; the other, that in countries having an advanced state of industrialization, the trend toward nationalization and governmental control has been arrested and even reversed. From this we are entitled to draw a new conclusion, somewhat different from the picture of socialism as the wave of the future, which was so easily accepted during the Great Depression, and which still pervades many parts of the world. The correct picture seems to be this: In early stages of economic development, a strong governmental hand is today not only desirable but inevitable. However, it is a mistake for the newer economies to conclude from this that socialism therefore has some kind of universal and eternal validity, merely because it happens to suit the particular stage of development they are in. They should also be prepared for the second half of the proposition, which is that, if they want to achieve the highest efficiency in the later stages of their development, they should not consider themselves bound by doctrinaire Socialist conceptions which may have worked at earlier stages.

The increased adoption even in the Soviet Union of incentives, productivity principles, managerial practices, price and profit devices, and other techniques borrowed from private enterprise reinforces the conclusion that a complex industrial economy cannot be run by decree. As the Soviet economy turns more and more toward consumer and even luxury goods, the difficulty of controlling distribution and production, as well as application of manpower, materials, and capital, by decree rather than by market, will become compounded. Therefore, there is every reason to look for a constant movement of the Soviet economy in the direction of Western economies, as it approaches their degree of consumer-based motivation.

The direct relevance of these points to the question of the idea struggle in the warless world is this: It is time that most people of the Western world got rid of the idea, once and for all, that there may be some little morsel of truth in the Communist boast that socialism is necessarily the wave of the future. If they could once assure themselves of the real truth, which is that the inherent nature and necessities of an industrial economy relentlessly force such an economy away from doctrinaire socialism, and that the temporary necessity for a strong government hand in newly developing economies is not inconsistent with this principle, they could face the nonviolent economic, political, and ideological competition of a warless world with quiet confidence.

The third revolution generated in the Atlantic Community is of a somewhat different type. This is the biological revolution leading to the rapid increase in population around the world. The occasion for attributing this revolution to the Atlantic Community is simply the advances in medicine and nutrition which have spread to other parts of the world and have prevented the operation of the ancient regulators of population: famine and pestilence.

The Western community and the Soviet Union have somewhat different ideas on what to do about the population problem, the former contending that large scale corrective measures are indicated, particularly in the poorer parts of the world, while the latter brush the problem aside, saying that we could feed all the people the world can produce if only we had general and complete disarmament and used all the resources so released to exploit new sources of food through science. Since the population problem is dealt with elsewhere in this book, only a brief comment need be made here. The Soviet idea, while it makes attractive and dramatic reading, seems a little remote from the everyday, clamoring realities of hunger and misery. To tell undernourished countries about a millennium in which everyone will have plenty to eat because of the extraction of food from the sea, the irrigation of deserts with desalinated sea water, and the like, is somewhat reminiscent of putting off the expectations of consumers in Communist countries with promises of the utopia to come when the Communist plan is more fully worked out. Most countries are no more apt to be satisfied by one than by the other, and for this reason the views of the newly developing countries are apt to be more closely identified with those of the Western countries on this point than with those of the Communists.

The fourth revolution is that of the application of science to human affairs. There is little that needs to be said on this point, since obviously the Soviet Union has joined this revolution with the greatest enthusiasm, and the total result for all the world of the advancement of science in all its aspects by Communist and non-Communist countries alike can only be beneficial, once we rule out the application of science to human destruction.

So far we have seen that the four great revolutions going on in the world, which were originated in the Atlantic Community, would for the most part find the Western nations and the newly developing countries closely aligned in a warless and disarmed world.

It has been noted in several chapters of this book that the end of war would not mean the end of human competition and struggle. Indeed, other forms of struggle might actually be intensified. Therefore it becomes important to ask where the advantage would lie, under the new rules of the game. In other words, who is most skilled and most experienced at the kinds of competition that will remain?

In answering this question, we must remember that the creation of the kind of world order assumed here carries with it more consequences than the mere absence of violence. For example, since no single nation would have the military power to defy the community of nations, it follows that rules and principles of international law could be expected to be enforced more directly and consistently than ever before.

The effect of this on the world propaganda struggle is particularly important. It has been demonstrated in a recent book * that the more dangerous forms of international propaganda by a state, including warmongering propaganda, subversive propaganda, and defamatory propaganda, are clearly illegal under international law, and that various remedies are available if the world community wishes to use them.

In the kind of warless world here assumed, it would be normal for such rules of international law to be obeyed and enforced. The consequence would be that the kind of lies, distortions, and half truths which we charge others with telling about us could be more effectively dealt with than they are now. The declared policy of the U. S. Information Agency and of the British Broadcasting Corporation is to stick to the truth. If, therefore, everyone in the warless world could be made to stick more closely to the truth, it is a truism to say that this would be great gain for the cause of truth.

Moreover, since the idea of a world of law, in which disputes are settled on the basis of right rather then might, is one to which the Western countries are deeply committed, it would also be a great gain generally if justiciable disputes were methodically handled by a judicial and arbitral settlement, as the United Nations Charter contemplates, instead of by power politics, as is now too often the case.

Again, since in a warless world any nation will have to rely much more on the kind of parliamentary procedures familiar to democratic countries, it would seem to follow that nations skilled in these procedures would enjoy a considerable advantage over

* *Propaganda: Towards Disarmament in the War of Words,* Arthur Larson and John B. Whitton, Oceana Press, 1963.

nations which have become accustomed to getting results in other ways.

One of the reasons for confusion on the prospects of the "idea struggle" is that the Western nations have never quite made up their minds about what it is that they are for in this struggle.

Painful as it may be, we should clear the decks by ruling out two or three of our most cherished values as absolute standards to be applied to other countries.

One is the idea of democracy. Of course we are in favor of democracy and want all people to enjoy its privileges. But this is quite a different matter from saying that any country which does not have a representative democratic form of government is outside the pale so far as we are concerned. The roots of this latter idea go back many years, and the idea still has some prevalence. For example, Woodrow Wilson believed that only democracies should be entitled to be members of the League of Nations. However, the experience of the past seventeen years has made it clear that the newly independent countries cannot be expected to embark upon parliamentary or Jeffersonian democracies, complete with fully developed representative assemblies, two-party political systems, and all the rest. How this is supposed to be managed in a country like the Congo, for example, which had seventeen college graduates and twenty identifiable political factions on its Independence Day, has never been explained. We have seen one fledgling theoretical democracy after another give way to strong-man regimes of some kind. There are many countries lacking democratic government that we consider responsible and friendly, and therefore, while of course we should continue to work for democracy wherever it is possible, its presence or absence is not of the essence in the idea struggle.

Even such a precious concept as "freedom" must be used with caution here. If by "freedom" we mean an insistence upon fully developed human and civil rights in every new country as the price of our approval, we are again going to be doomed to many disappointments.

What then is of the essence? The clue to the answer lies in

the fact that we are here concerned with international, not internal, conduct. So far as internal affairs are concerned, as a matter of United Nations Charter principles, international law, and ancient custom, no nation has the right to interfere in the internal affairs of another. Therefore, when we are dealing with such matters as internal political democracy, civil and human rights of individuals, and economic arrangements, while we are entitled to use all of the devices of persuasion, example, education, economic aid, and political pressure that are short of illegal interference, we have no right to go further and attempt to demand or impose internal standards. So far as these internal matters are concerned, we can only proceed on the faith that, aided by such legitimate measures, in most instances our common interests, and even a common ideological denominator like the Lincoln formula, will eventually bring us out on the same side of most questions as most of the nations of the world.

But so far as international conduct is concerned, when we have removed force and armaments as an arbiter of international conduct, we have not only the right but the duty to insist that certain standards be observed. One may conclude, then, with the suggestion that there are ultimately only two standards which must be a test of the right of a nation to be a member of the civilized community of nations. These two precepts are: respect your international obligations; and do not molest your neighbors.

If we can achieve the acceptance of these two principles in a warless world, there is a good chance that a warless world could succeed, and that in the endless struggle of ideas going on within this framework, the great ideas which have built modern civilization could be made to survive and prosper.

# X

## Psychological problems of warlessness

BY JUDD MARMOR

Clinical Professor of Psychiatry,
University of California at Los Angeles

Underlying all of the propositions of this book is a serious question. Is the personality of man capable of functioning without the outlet of war? Is war so deeply and inexorably a part of man's basic nature that all talk of a world without war must be relegated, reluctantly but hardheadedly, to the waste basket of utopian, wishful thinking? It is to this question that I wish to address myself first.

The assumption that war is an intrinsic manifestation of human nature grows out of the theory that it is an inevitable social expression of fundamental instinct toward destructive aggression in man. I shall not attempt here to review the pro and con arguments with regard to this theory, other than to indicate that its validity has been seriously questioned by numerous social and biological scientists. As Fairfield Osborn has pointed out: "Warfare as practiced by man has no parallel in nature.... Within the more highly developed animal populations of the earth there is not now nor has there ever been similar destruction within a species itself. In fact one has to go to the lowliest forms of animals, such as certain kinds of ants, to find anything comparable to human warfare."

Most modern behavioral scientists believe that human violence is not spontaneously instinctive, but rather a *reactive response* either to a sense of frustration or to perceived threats involving some aspect of man's psychological or physical security. This latter view does not deny that the *capacity* for violence is innate in man but asserts that whether or not this capacity is *expressed,* generally depends on external factors.

The crucial point for our discussion, however, is that even if one were to concede, for the sake of argument, that aggression *is* an innate human instinct, it still would not follow logically that wars are inevitable. It is meaningless to talk of modern war as though it were merely the sum total of countless individual human aggressions. Modern war is a complicated social institution—the resultant of the intermeshing of many intricate factors: social, economic, political, and psychological. It involves large and complex social organizations which we call nations. It requires armies, weapons, supplies, scientific research, advanced technology, recruitment, and propaganda. Like any other social institution, it is capable of evolution and change. It is precisely its evolution from the techniques of primitive hand-to-hand combat to those of modern nuclear annihilation which confronts the world with its current awesome danger. As a social institution, however, it is also potentially eradicable. Other widespread social institutions of man's past, like slavery, dueling, ritual human sacrifice, and cannibalism, which in their times and milieus seemed equally rooted in human nature and destiny, have been, in the course of history, almost totally eliminated. It is also a fact that various societies have existed without recourse to war for many generations.

But even though it seems incontrovertible that war is not an inevitable expression of human nature, there are certain aspects of human psychology which strongly predispose man to violence, and which require consideration, since they would be operative even in a warless world.

Perhaps the most fundamental of these, although not necessarily the most important, is *fear.* Abundant clinical experience has shown that panic is a highly potent trigger for hostile behavior, and extreme fear of an adversary is as likely to provoke a violent act as is hatred of him. Yet fear is a basic biological reaction without which an individual might fail to take the proper actions needed for his protection and survival in the face of danger. Unfortunately, however, there is only a thin line between the amount of fear necessary to stimulate corrective behavior and the amount that leads to maladaptive responses. Psychologists have long been aware of what has been called the *primitivizing effect of fear*. The reactions of humans, no less than those of animals, tend to become more archaic and less rational under conditions of extreme fear or panic. The capacity for adaptive discrimination is lost and habitual responses which are no longer appropriate are fallen back upon. When fire breaks out in a theater, for example, most people will rush for the main exits even though they are already jammed with people, and will ignore the more passable but less customary exits. In the same way, when fears of an adversary are fanned to great heights by communication media, an unbearable tension is created in many people—tension which seeks relief at nearly any cost. Under such stress, almost any course may seem better than none at all. Hence the cry, so often heard, for "action" and "getting it over with," even though such action might be self-defeating or self-destructive. The certainties of war at such times may appear more endurable than the ambiguities of peace. Fear also shortens time perspectively. A fearful person becomes preoccupied with warding off the imminent danger, often to the neglect of the ultimate consequences of his behavior. Similarly, nations may counter what they perceive as an immediate threat by the adversary, with action involving long-term consequences which may be much more serious than the initial hazard.

It follows, then, that even in a warless world anything which aroused intense or prolonged fear in people would favor the outbreak of group violence. The elimination of weapons of mass destruction would, of course, remove one of the main potential sources of such panic. Other factors, however, would still remain.

Perhaps the most serious of these are the mutual distortions of perception which tend to occur between the populations of nations in conflict. These distortions can be subsumed under the general concept of *ethnocentric perception*. This refers to the tendency of members of a group to perceive and evaluate events from the standpoint of their own group's interest and bias. The virtues of one's own side are magnified and its faults are not seen, while the evils of the adversary are exaggerated and his virtues ignored. Thus the identical behavior which is perceived as "standing firm" when exhibited by a member of one's own group, is interpreted as "being pigheaded and obstinate" when manifested by a member of the opposing group.

This often leads to *stereotyped* conceptions, both of one's self and of the adversary, with the development of a self-righteous view of the ingroup and a bogey-man view of the opponent. The motives of one's own group are always assumed to be morally honorable, fair, and decent; those of the opposing group are always suspect.

Ethnocentric perception also favors the development of *polarized attitudes,* in which everything is regarded as black or white, never as gray. All truth and morality are regarded as being on one side, all deceit and evil on the other. All who are not 100 per cent on one's own side are regarded as being on the opponent's side, and neutrality is viewed with suspicion and hostility. Differences with the adversary tend to be exaggerated and similarities to be minimized.

It should not be assumed that ethnocentric perception is necessarily a matter of faulty access to information or of faulty intelligence. Although its extreme manifestations are more apt to be observed among people with lesser educational backgrounds, it occurs in greater or lesser degree among almost all people, in high stations as well as low ones, and even among those who have access to the widest sources of information. The reason for this is rooted in the homeostatic need of all human beings to organize their perceptions to fit into their pre-existent conscious and unconscious expectations, needs, and wishes, and to reject, minimize, or "fail to see" things that would upset their basic views about the nature of reality. This is an effort to keep the environment as constant and as meaningful as possible, and to avoid whatever might make it appear disturbing or unclear. This "intolerance of ambiguity" or "need for certainty" increases whenever individuals feel threatened, and tends to lessen with feelings of emotional security.

Another basic aspect of human psychology which is involved in ethnocentric distortions is the *tendency to modify one's per-*

*ceptions and reactions in response to group pressures.* The effect of mob hysteria on individual behavior is a well-known phenomenon, but the ways in which more subtle group pressures affect people often are not as well recognized. This phenomenon was strikingly illustrated by an ingenious psychological experiment in which a subject is placed in a group of six or eight others all of whom are asked to make certain perceptual or evaluative judgments. What the subject does not know is that the experiment is rigged, that the others have all been instructed to give *false* responses on a predetermined schedule. At first the subject finds himself in agreement with the others, but then finds his responses differing from *all* the others more and more often. He is at first puzzled, then gets more and more upset, begins to doubt his own judgment, and finally, in about one third of the cases, begins actually to "see" things the way the others presumably do! There is little doubt that this kind of unconsciously influenced perception takes place very widely in all countries, particularly when a conflict with an outside group increases the nationalistic pressures toward conformity.

All of these distortions inevitably lead to a *biased perception of what is fair and reasonable,* and thus not only render meaningful negotiations between adversaries difficult and sometimes impossible, but also fan the winds of fear and hate in their respective populations. The *mutual distrust* that inevitably develops under such circumstances becomes itself one of the most serious of the obstacles to nonviolent resolution of the conflicts between nations. The expectation that no agreement can be reached because "the other side doesn't really want peace" and "can't be trusted" inevitably leads to the anticipated failure and thus becomes a self-fulfilling prophecy.

Finally, no discussion of the psychological obstacles to nonviolence in international conflict can ignore the significant *interactions that exist between heads of governments and their peoples.* Many of the perceptual distortions of an adversary's actions and purposes are often deliberately created and manipulated by political leaders through the withholding of significant information or the dissemination of false information for the purpose of achieving certain strategic objectives in the power struggle with the adversary. Also things may be said by them which are intended only for domestic consumption and domestic power politics but which lend themselves to misinterpretation by the adversary. Once this has been done, however, the tensions, fears, and hostilities created in the minds of their populations become potent forces in themselves which control the subsequent freedom of the leaders to act. Thus a constant dialectical interplay exists between national leaders and their followers which often makes both of them captives of a vicious cycle of increasing tensions. This is particularly true in open societies like our own, but the significance of such interactions should not be minimized even in Communist societies. Consequently, even when leaders may wish to make realistic compromises with the adversary, they may be unable to do so because of nationalistic pressures, the dictates of political expediency, the influence of power blocs within their own country, and the fears and suspicions that have already been aroused among their own peoples.

We see then that the psychological obstacles to the elimination of organized violence are formidable indeed. Is it possible to modify these barriers or else to find other outlets for them in a world without war? What kinds of psychological changes will be necessary for man to live in such a world without propelling himself once more in the direction of violent internecine conflict with his fellow man?

The first word of caution that needs to be introduced is the reminder that a warless world does not mean a world without conflict. Conflict between individuals, groups, and nations will always be part of the human scene as long as there are diversities of human interests and values. Peace is not a static end-point; it is a dynamic, on-going process of continuous conflict resolution. Moreover, conflict per se is not necessarily evil. It may have, and often does have, constructive value. The mobilization of energy toward conflict-resolution can have integrative and creative value for a nation as well as for an individual. One of the challenges of a warless world is to enable people and nations to learn to engage in conflict without violence—to find, in William James's apt phrase, the "moral equivalents of war."

That this is psychologically possible for man there can be little doubt. Man has shown himself capable of finding adequate discharge for his aggressive and competitive impulses in all kinds of peacetime activities short of violence. However, many unhealthy current social mores may have to be altered if man's present tendency to erupt into violence is to be significantly modified.

Much has been written, for example, in recent years, about the social and psychological effects of population increases, industrialization, specialization, urbanization, and automation on people. The effect with which I am specifically concerned here is the deindividualization and alienation of man—an alienation which brings with it a sense of noninvolvement and indifference to the actual or potential distress of other human beings and thus has a bearing on the capacity of people psychologically to tolerate the implications of mass destruction and mass violence. As a result of this process man becomes regarded as a cost factor, an item, or a tool to serve the organization or the mass machine. He becomes a means to an end, rather than an end in itself. In the semantics of modern military strategy, patterns of thinking are often observable which reflect this dehumanization of man. Concepts such as "first-strike," "overkill," "counterforce deterrence," and so on, represent a move-countermove, game-theory type of thinking which treats the millions of potential human victims as mere statistics or pawns in a global chess game, and psychologically screens out the awesome consequences of the contemplated actions upon individual people—a full appreciation of which would make such actions emotionally intolerable.

One must recognize, however, that the effects of modern technology, automation, and even bureaucracy have not by any means been merely negative. They have also had enormously constructive effects in promoting efficiency, in relieving human drudgery and strain, and in making possible a richer life and increased leisure time for more people. Moreover, intertwined with the trends toward conformity and anonymity in modern society, there are also present persistent impulses toward individuation—in art, in literature, and in the tenacious strivings of men everywhere toward goals of freedom, peace, and human dignity.

Nevertheless, the pressures of modern technology are likely to continue the trend toward the deindividuation of man, and there will be urgent need, in a warless world, to develop psychic antidotes of "rehumanization" to counteract the heightened callousness and the lessened sense of personal responsibility toward the needs or suffering of other human beings which such a trend brings with it.

Still another problem with which a warless world would have to deal would be that of the conceptual stereotypes concerning war which are deeply rooted in our language and traditions, and which foster attitudes conducive to group violence. The history books of every nation justify its wars as brave, righteous, and honorable. This glorification is charged with overtones of patriotism and love of country. Virtues such as heroism and courage are regarded as being "manly" and are traditionally associated with waging war. Conversely, the avoidance of war or the pursuit of peace are generally regarded as "effeminate," passive, cowardly, weak, dishonorable, or subversive. The brutal realities of war are glamorized and obscured in countless tales of heroism and glory, and the warnings of an occasional General Sherman that "War is hell . . . its glory is all moonshine" receive little or no mention.

One of the fundamental points at which a warless society might begin to deal with these stereotypes is in the kinds of influences to which its children are exposed. We often hear it said, for example, that war games and military toys are good for children—that they serve as outlets for their aggressive feelings. It may well be true that they serve as such outlets, but they also prepare the soil for a psychological acceptance of war and violence. One could justify them only if no other kind of toy or game were available which could serve equally well as an outlet for aggressive impulses—an assumption which is patently untrue. The same argument holds in my opinion with regard to the show of violence in TV, movies, and comic strips. The oft-heard defense that such violence is merely a mirror of "what goes on in the child's unconscious, anyway," and that "healthy, well-adjusted children" are not adversely affected by it, fails to pose the problem in proper perspective. Even if it were true—and it is by no means a proven fact—that aggressive impulses are endogenous and spontaneous in young children, the *forms* and the *outlets* such impulses take are modifiable. There is nothing in the human unconscious which instinctively endows it with the knowledge of "civilized" techniques of torture or killing. To teach children such techniques via our mass-communication media is not only to indoctrinate them in methods of brutality but also to progressively desensitize them to the spectacle of human death and violence. This, it seems to me, is a much more serious problem, from the standpoint of society, than whether or not such forms of "entertainment" do or do not cause emotional disturbances in some children. If the organized killing of men is to be rendered obsolete, it is not enough to pay lip service to nonviolence in terms of our religious mores, when so many other aspects of our social fabric condone or even glorify such killing. To be consistent, every element in the acculturation process which shapes our perceptions and our goals should reinforce the value systems of nonviolence, beginning in early childhood and continuing throughout life. Not only the toys and games of childhood, but our textbooks, our history books, our encyclopedias, and our mass-communications media need to be oriented toward the ennoblement of man's peaceful accomplishments rather than the glamorization of his battles. Our scientists, our educators, and our creative artists, not our generals, need to be the heroes of history.

It may be argued that what I am advocating is a kind of massive indoctrination of people that is incompatible with the ideals of a free society. Such an argument fails to take into account the fact that no society is without a set of mores which it imposes on its members, either implicitly or explicitly. The glorification of military action has been precisely such a value system. It developed out of the historical necessities of international relationships at a time in which the instrument of armed force appeared to be the only way of achieving urgent national goals. The fact is that we have now entered upon an era in which the resort to war can no longer serve this purpose. In the face of this development it becomes imperative for man, if he is to survive, to consciously alter the outmoded value systems which serve to make war psychologically palatable and to replace them with others which have greater adaptive usefulness. To endeavor to plan our educational, child-training, and mass-communication systems along principles which enhance the dignity and worth of human life is not merely a social necessity in our nuclear age, but also compatible with the most cherished values of a free society.

A world without war may well find it necessary to re-examine others of its values in the light of these criteria. One would expect, for example, that traditional attitudes of punitiveness and vindictiveness toward juvenile delinquents, drug addicts, and criminals would give way increasingly to patterns emphasizing their treatment and rehabilitation; and that the ultimate expression of society's violence toward the individual—capital punishment—would become progressively rarer.

However, even if the predisposition to acts of individual violence could be reduced—as I believe it can be—by such modifications in our acculturation processes, what can be done to eliminate the ethnocentric biases which tend to foster *group* attitudes of violence and hatred between nations who are at odds with one another? Here we have to deal with another significant set of stereotypes which will require changing—those associated with nationalism. As Stagner reminds us, "Three hundred years ago suggestions of religious tolerance were denounced as evidences of moral weakness. Today we consider religious *intolerance* a sign of moral decay. . . . We may reach a point at which the delusions of national pride and national persecution will be looked upon in the same way."

The elimination of patterns of nationalistic bias does *not* mean the elimination of love of country. A man does not love his family less because he has a deep love of his country; nor does he love his country less because he has a deep feeling for humanity as a whole. But just as a man's love for his family is transcended by his loyalty to his nation if the latter's existence should be threatened, so also it is possible and imperative for a man's love of his country to be transcended by his loyalty to the whole human race, if *its* existence is threatened, be it by natural catastrophe, pandemic disease, or total war. Indeed, one psychological way of assessing man's emotional maturity is in terms of his capacity to transcend his parochial attachments. When we are very young we love only our parents and our immediate family. As we grow, we must become able to move out of the tight little circle of family attachments and to love people who are outside of it. Persons who are emotionally immature are unable to do this, and can love only people who are very much like themselves or like the significant members of their family. Such individuals, we say, have "failed to resolve their Oedipus complex" or are capable only of a kind of "narcissistic" love. Indirect reflections of such immaturity can be seen in those adults who remain excessively involved with such in-group symbols as their fraternities, their sororities, their college football team, or the state of Texas, and are unable to make close attachments to persons outside of their particular extended family groups. The more emotionally mature an individual becomes, the more he becomes able to love others on the basis of their actual merits as people, and not just because they come from the same home town, belong to the same lodge, go to the same church, or have the same color skin that he has. In this sense, the capacity to transcend nationalistic feelings when the welfare of humanity itself is involved represents a higher level of emotional development. This value system receives implicit recognition when we label such great humanitarians as Albert Schweitzer and Eleanor Roosevelt "citizens of the world." It is not only psychologically possible, but essential if man is to survive, for the inhabitants of all nations ultimately to demonstrate adherence to an international law which will transcend their own national laws whenever the welfare of the world is involved, just as the people in the fifty states of our Union generally accept the fact that Federal law supersedes their own whenever the national welfare is involved. Signs of such a trend are already apparent in the slowly increasing tendency of many sovereign states to delegate certain powers to the United Nations, or to other international trade or monetary organizations.

But if conflict between nations persists, as it is likely to do over one issue or another, is it psychologically feasible that it can be pursued without violence? There is an accumulating body of evidence to indicate that the nonviolent pursuit of conflict between groups is not only feasible but can actually be very effective. Where traditional approaches of diplomacy, negotiation, or mediation have failed, other techniques such as sanctions or boycotts are still available short of war. The active but nonviolent techniques of carrying on conflict as practiced under the leadership of such men as Gandhi and Martin Luther King are illustrative of the tremendous moral power inherent in such ways of dealing with an adversary; and although not directly applicable to the current East-West conflict, might become more relevant in a world in which the use of lethal mass weapons has been outlawed. Such methods of struggle not only tend to contribute to the restoration of the humanistic values upon which Western civilization prides itself, but also serve to correct the distorted psychological stereotypes which exist concerning violence. For the nonviolent fighter, resort to violence is a sign of weakness, while adherence to nonviolence is a demonstration of inner strength and courage. Psychologically this has considerable validity. Psychiatrists have long known that the resort to violence stems more often from feelings of fear and inner weakness than from strength, and that the customary "common sense" equation of violence with strength and nonviolence with weakness is often a false one in terms of unconscious psychodynamics.

Psychiatrists have also learned that efforts to control an angry patient with force almost always make him violent in return, while the avoidance of violence tends to inhibit such reactions in him. It has been demonstrated repeatedly that it is possible to set up group standards in a hospital ward which, even under great provocation, will preclude the use of violence by both patients and staff.

At the level of international conflict some fundamentally different approaches are also worth considering. The great dilemma of our time is that we seem to be faced with an irreconcilable conflict between two powerful ideological, political, and economic systems, yet any effort to seek a military solution can result only in mutual annihilation. History has taught us that often the only way out of a dilemma of this kind lies in a critical re-examination of the customary modes of thought out of which it grew. Some of the fundamental paradoxes in the field of natural science, for example, were resolved only when habitual common-sense ways of thinking about time and space were transcended by the new modes of thought in Einstein's theory of relativity. Similarly, many paradoxes of human behavior remained obscure until Freud's insight into the existence of unconscious processes was able to clarify what common-sense approaches had not been able to. The traditional mode of thinking about international conflicts is in terms of a struggle for power with the only possible ultimate outcome being victory of one side over the other, and finds expression in the "Red or dead" formula which has such wide currency. The leap in our thinking which is necessary to resolve this dilemma is to recognize that it is possible for adversaries to compete with one another *without necessarily encompassing the destruction of either one. Indeed in the process of the competition both sides may even grow stronger.* This implies an acceptance of coexistence which many people on both sides of the struggle find extremely unpalatable. Yet the hard fact is that in our nuclear era there is no alternative but to face and accept this. Actually, such coexistence between great ideological adversaries is not alien to human experience. After centuries of futile and bloody violence, Christianity and Mohammedanism settled down to living side by side, and even within Christianity itself, the competitive coexistence of Protestantism and Catholicism is taken for granted. The Ecumenical Council is an interesting illustration of the fact that given enough time, in the absence of violence, dialectical forces are often set into motion which eventually tend to bring adversaries closer together. Even in the current ideological struggle there is evidence in recent years of a trend toward democratization in the Soviet Union which seems to increase as its sense of security increases but diminishes when it feels threatened.

Cooperation between adversaries represents still another nontraditional approach to conflict resolution which tends to be emotionally rejected by many people. The idea that it is possible to collaborate with an opponent, particularly one whose fundamental ideology is so antithetical to our own, appears at first glance to be utterly naïve. Yet, as Thomas Schelling of Harvard, author of "The Strategy of Conflict," has pointed out, some co-operation between the opposing sides took place even in World Wars I and II, when their mutual interests were involved.

Cooperative activities yield rewards which reinforce positive attitudes between adversaries and inhibit antagonistic ones. Particularly effective are cooperative endeavors toward mutually desired or needed superordinate goals which neither side can achieve alone, such as the researches during the International Geophysical Year. Such activities also include a competitive component which can serve as a healthy channel for national rivalries. Other potentially constructive competitions in a warless world would exist in the race toward the exploration of space, in the arts and sciences, and in the rivalry of the great nations to help the underdeveloped nations of the world.

I realize that I have not attempted to project into the future the utopian potentialities which exist for man psychologically in a world without war. If I have not done so, it is not because I do not believe that such potentialities exist, but because I think it is first necessary to try to understand some of the more immediate psychological problems with which he may be faced in the transitional period in trying to preserve the precious peace that he will have attained. In attempting this, I have no illusions that in this limited presentation I have been able to touch upon more than a fraction of these problems. There is no doubt that they will be many and complex. However, the remarkable brain of man, which has unleashed the secret of the atom and is solving the mysteries of space, is fully capable of coping with them. Most people on our planet yearn consciously for a world at peace; but man's unconscious irrationality may yet destroy him in spite of his conscious wishes. One of the major goals of behavioral science is to increase man's self-understanding so as to bring his unconscious attitudes and impulses under conscious control. Never was such a goal more imperative than in today's world, lest the very machines which man in his ingenuity has constructed, become through his folly, the monsters which encompass his destruction.

# XI

## The psychology of warless man

BY MARGARET MEAD

Anthropologist, Associate Curator of Ethnology,
American Museum of Natural History

The establishment of a warless world must be viewed in a strict contemporary light. Whatever can be said now, after the development of totally destructive thermonuclear, biological, and chemical warfare, differs profoundly from anything that was or might have been said in any earlier period of history either about the beauties of peace or about the horrors of war and its positive by-products—patriotism, bravery, and radical innovation. We must realize clearly how the total context has changed from that envisaged as recently as the beginning of World War II, if we are to appreciate fully our present situation and the rewards that can be reaped by the abolishment of war. Poets and prophets have longed for peace and have extolled it. Religious groups have been formed to work for peace. But these past activities are now essentially peripheral. Even the warlike have always recognized periods without war as desirable. The exhausted have sought for truces, and those who have preferred a quiet life have welcomed them. But once man had invented the idea of warfare, it was certain that there would be new wars as long as some people, some of the time, could benefit by them. Warfare is a system in which the unwilling and the unready are just as firmly enmeshed as are the willing and the ready.

But now, for the first time in human history, war profits no man. There can be no victor and no vanquished. And now, for the first time, we have a genuine opportunity to establish a world-wide rule of law and order. In the past, when men spoke of peace, what they meant in fact was a truce. The Pax Romanum, the Pax Britannica were no more than a condition within a single system. As long as it was not to every nation's benefit to belong within one system, we could not effectively conceive of such a system and we could not really speak of peace. But even now, when a warless world is within our reach—because the alternative is, potentially, complete destruction—peace remains a vague and too inclusive word.

I shall address myself to the kinds of moral and psychological change which we may reasonably expect in the post-Hiroshima period as a result of steps taken to bring about a warless world. By this I mean a world in which resort to force is no longer an acceptable method of resolving disagreements between groups organized as nations, liberation movements, separatist movements, and so on. Such a change does not carry with it, necessarily, any reduction in other forms of violence. Nor will the existence of a warless world, as such, protect men and the human race from other dangers, particularly from the uncontrolled, irresponsible application of science to man's environment, or the relations of man and man, or the relations of human group and human group.

Given a world in which there was effective disarmament and an effective political organization which made resort to warfare impossible, what would the moral and psychological consequences be?

The first great outcome would be a resoration of faith in the continuity of human life in all its rich and manifold forms, of faith in man, his civilizations, and his power to grow and change. Faith in continuity has been essential to the existence of all known societies. Men must believe that the sun will rise tomorrow, that summer follows winter, that the Pleiades and other constellations follow fixed paths across the sky, that the moon waxes and wanes and the tides respond, that where game has been found or fruit has grown it will be found again, that a seed planted in the ground will grow into a plant, which will in turn yield a seed, that a pregnant woman will in due time bear a child, that a child will grow into a man, and that all men and women age and die.

In other species, the behavior which is necessary for maintaining life—for guiding a group to food, for rearing and protecting the young—combines instinct and learning. Each small cue, a change in temperature or wind or light or form, sets off the next behavior. The hibernating bear is not asked to believe, "If Winter comes, can Spring be far behind?" It depends, instead, upon the cues given by the regularities in nature.

But man long ago shifted from an instinctive, day-by-day dependence on light and temperature and humidity to a dependence on his power to imagine, and describe in words, whatever was absent—the unborn babe, the flowering plant, the coming winter. For other creatures, continuity is provided by the complex ecological setting, in which their fate is determined by the balance of their own and other species and the long-term effects of climactic periodicity. But man has made his own world. He learned, and taught his children, that seed must be planted, gardens tended, and the harvest brought in; he learned when the fish would appear, when the herds of buffalo would sweep across the plains. No single part of the complex equipment which a human being needs in order to believe in and anticipate his own growth and to deal with the world, natural and man-made, is left to nature alone. All man's protective knowledge has become cultural—man-made and man-taught—and it is correspondingly fragile.

And men have always had difficulty in trusting their culturally built up beliefs in the future, their confidence in the dependable regularities of the world they were slowly learning to understand. From the young mother who tiptoes in to assure herself that her newborn baby is real, to the peoples who beat drums and make sacrifices, for fear the sun might disappear, when the sky darkens in an eclipse, men have had recurrent doubts. And recurrently, men's doubts have been fed by accidents, by ignorance, by false assumptions about the sequence of events.

But as men have gained mastery over nature through their ability to calculate distances in time and space, to understand natural sequences, and to invent the means of conquering hazards, from the earliest astrolabes to our modern warning systems that protect hundreds of thousands of lives in a severe hurricane, men's faith in the regularity of the natural world also has increased. In the modern world, wherever science was an integral part of experience, there was a tremendous upsweep of faith in the future. Ships could churn across the seas, airplanes could be guided to their destinations by instruments, blueprints could be drawn up for huge dams, a calendar of the moon's rising and setting could be printed for centuries ahead, drugs could give frail children the gift of life. Men's sense of continuity rose to a high point, and the need for magical or religious intervention in the routines of daily life dropped precipitously. Men still prayed for grace. But the desert blossomed as the rose, and soon it might not be necessary to pray for rain but only to resolve the conflicts between the farmer who wanted a real downpour and the baseball team that did not.

Then with staggering impact came the atom bomb, the hydrogen bomb, the intercontinental missile, the manned space ship, the implications of fallout for this and every future generation. From the very source from which man's faith in the continuity of human life had come, it was taken away. Within a single decade, human beings were asked to learn that all the assurance which was based on scientific knowledge had been shattered by the very knowledge in which they trusted. They had now to learn that there is no assurance of continuity, not even the fragile, hard-to-believe-in continuity of a single Eskimo family following wind marks in the snow.

This new crisis which mankind faces collectively, as all men now live in an intercommunicating world, is comparable only with the crisis which, over and over, small groups of men have had to face as each group has approached some understanding that death is natural—that individual death is neither an accident nor a punishment nor the outcome of a hostile act by some living being, but only a natural event. For millennia men have struggled to come to grips with this knowledge; most recently, as they have talked about the possibility of curing all disease, they have had to struggle with the implicit, irrational hope that death itself might be conquered.

At the very point in time when, whatever faith or hope men might have in immortality, in an afterlife or a reincarnation, the fact of death was fully accepted and the future was seen in the light of a disciplined reliance on science, man was suddenly faced with a threat far more terrible than that of individual death. Long ago, men learned to place their hopes in the children of their lineage or tribe or nation, in the enduring products of creative imagination—their buildings, their poems and paintings, and the faiths they initiated—and in the paeans of praise raised by those whose life and well-being their acts had made possible.

But now all hope, and with it all certainty, is placed in jeopardy. The threat is not that of individual death or the heroic sacrifice of a whole army or even the destruction of a civilian population, heroically patient under bombing; it is not the loss of country or the destruction of a civilization or even the annihilation of all the art and beauty man has made. It is *all* these things, together. In the past, the end of individual human life was made tolerable by the faith that some part at least of what a man valued would endure. But now this faith is threatened with extinction. Without a future for anyone, anywhere, human life loses its meaning. There is no rationale for the simplest act, no reason to save or to plan or to build; no reason to vote or to sit in committees; no reason to plant or to pray. As men see it, this new possibility of total destruction is not an act of God's vengeance turned against a particular unfaithful people but instead an act which is the outcome of man's fullest development as man.

A disarmed and ordered world would lift this fear, in its most acute form, from the hearts and minds of men. It would restore their full humanity by restoring, in a new form, their belief and trust in the future and so also their capacity to exercise their imagination. In a warless world, men would have time to come to grips with the terrible responsibilities of their new estate.

The one thing we cannot do is restore the past; the change brought about by our capacity to destroy ourselves is permanent. Monitoring for tests, destroying the actual bombs, ceasing to manufacture fissionable materials for the purposes of war—these are only absolutely essential steps to prevent immediate catastrophe. But the bomb, in the sense that it stands for man's newly acquired powers of destruction, is here to stay. The need for vigilance against the exercise of this power to destroy—to destroy the earth's food supply, to contaminate the atmosphere, to make the earth uninhabitable, to distort every infant born, to paralyze men's wills—this will be no less present in a warless world. In the foreseeable future, the tapping of virtually inexhaustible supplies of physical energy can make it unnecessary for men to earn their bread by the sweat of their brow. This will not alter the necessity, in the foreseeable future, of protecting all living things from the human species' own scientifically acquired and based powers of destruction. But in a world from which the pall of fear has been lifted, men's minds will be freed to meet this new requirement.

Beside the tremendous consequences of restoring to mankind a trust in the continuity of life, the other by-products of the abolition of war pale to insignificance.

The abolition of war would resolve the age-long conflict between the admonition that it is wrong to kill another human being and the belief that it is right to kill an enemy. As long as warfare was little more than a running feud between two small groups, gratification of the desire for prestige and satisfaction of the impulse of revenge through fighting and killing could be safely enough built into the character of the headhunter, the warrior, the loyal member of a family or a band. But as the scale of civilization increased, warfare necessarily became increasingly impersonal. Organized invocations of their imagination bound men to fellow subjects or fellow citizens whom they had never met. Impersonal symbolic ideas defined not only those who were their enemies and might be killed by sword or spear, by Greek fire or battering ram, by swift attack or slow relentless siege. And in a world in which one's fellows and one's enemies must be numbered in the hundreds of millions, there can be no real relationship between man's individual aggressive response to the threatening posture of another male (whatever this may once have been) and the requirement of killing an enemy, personally unknown and unseen, located perhaps a hundred or a thousand miles away. Nevertheless, man still retains his ability to translate into deeply meaningful symbols his primitive impulse to protect his women and his children as well as to symbolize the threat which men, unknown to him as persons, present to his women and his children, his home, his country, his religion, his highest values.

It would seem that the intractable element in human nature which has been involved through the ages in organized warfare is just this blind, sacrificial willingness to defend what one values —at any cost. Large, modern states have more or less effectively disciplined the human impulse to settle individual differences and disputes and to right individual wrongs, by fist fighting or knifing or dueling or shooting. But far from curbing man's impulse to fight for whatever he holds dear, modern states have gone to great lengths to create sets of symbols which will be dependably effective in rousing the willingness to defend one's own.

This means that warfare, especially warfare in which the total population is involved, is based not on man's impulse to destroy but on his desire to protect. This makes the problem of how to establish psychological equivalences for war a much easier one. For every society—and a world-wide society more than any other—depends for its continued existence on the active vigilance and the cherishing care of its citizens.

In fact, the new powers which science has put into men's hands require new and more difficult forms of vigilance—more complex, more organized, more exacting. A Manus man who wanted to protect his pregnant wife from eating food cooked on a fire made of wood, which was taboo to her, had an easy task in comparison with that of the modern man who is trying to protect his wife and unborn child from the unknown dangers of some new and as yet little-tried drug. The Manus man had only to watch over his fire and his own wife's coming and going. But to protect his wife and child, the modern man must involve himself in activities that concern the welfare of all the women not only of his country but also of the whole intercommunicating world.

This will require an even greater use of symbolization. But since we have already been able to educate human beings to regard hundreds of millions of persons, few of whom they will ever see, as fellow citizens or as enemies, we have reason to believe it will be possible to extend our symbolic loyalties to include the whole human race. Research has shown that individuals differ enormously in the number of actual persons with whom they can maintain close contact. This does not mean, however, that symbolic interaction—among fellow Americans, among fellow citizens of the Soviet Union, among all the members of the British Commonwealth—does not take place and cannot be expanded indefinitely. But there is, of course, the danger that symbolic hostility, based on no physical reality of personal experience, can just as readily be enlarged to include ever-larger segments of mankind.

One probable predictable effect of the removal of the ever-present threat of war may be an increase in other kinds of organized aggression. For war not only used violence as its sanction, it also served as a sanction against violence. This specter of external attack has frequently served to muffle sectional disputes, just as a quarrel between two members of a group is muted in the face of some attack upon the group as a whole. As yet, it is impossible to estimate the extent to which the idea of a common, shared anger acts to support group solidarity. Group solidarity, is, of course, not entirely dependent on a belief in its effectiveness in averting threats of war, but the threat of war is one element in averting the outbreak of internal conflict. It is important to recognize, therefore, that the creation of an international police force, whose duty it will be to prevent the kind of conflict that once was settled by war, may have very little effect in muting the kinds of conflict that far from leading to war actually were prevented by war or a continuing fear of war. Within national states —and today even within larger regions—the clash of interests between management and labor or agriculture, between rival trade unions or rival producer organizations, between rival fishing fleets or rival air lines can lead to conflicts which governments have held down quite effectively in wartime and less effectively in peacetime; and, unless measures are taken to control them, such conflicts may well increase rather than abate with the abolition of war between states.

This is not because human beings have a given quantum of aggression and hostility which must find an outlet in some form. It is rather because, as nations have been built up, the national interest, expressed in terms of the dangers from external enemies to which all members of the nation are exposed, has been included as one important element in local peace-keeping structures. In particular, the abolition of war will give men no protection against such dissident organizations as the Irish Republican Army or the Organization de l'Armée Secrete nor will it protect citizen groups against the violence of certain types of government action. The very success of efforts to bring about a warless world will necessitate innovations in internal, local peace-keeping structures.

It is also quite possible that there may be an increase in individual acts of violence. This is particularly likely in the period immediately after disarmament when it will be necessary to cope with a generation who were reared to respond with extreme partisanship and unconcealed hostility to special symbols standing for friend and foe, our values and their values. The years since World War II have been marked by a sharply mounting number of small, dangerous acts of anarchy—terrorist bombings and bombs hidden in civilian planes, the formation of secret subversive organizations, the piratical seizure of ships and planes, "invasions" by fleets of ten motor launches, etc. In part it has been difficult to bring such activities under control because, in the precarious state of nuclear armaments and competition among power blocs, it is believed that active intervention by any of the great powers might trigger a nuclear war. The state of nuclear blackmail encouraged small-scale anarchy.

It is equally probable that the administrators of a warless world, preoccupied by the problems of putting into effect the controls designed to maintain world peace, may be relatively impotent to control acts of individual or small group violence directed to minor political and criminal ends. Most countries have resorted to one or another form of internal military action to keep such activities in check. But dissident factions in a nation's armed forces sometimes have initiated or supported anarchical activities, and others have been kept under control by an overriding *esprit de corps.* The dangers of individual violence may be increased by the dissimilarities in experience among the member nation-states. Some will have in their populations many men who know of no life other than that of arms; some will be less than a generation away from tribal raiding or border warfare; some will include minority groups who are just beginning to assert their rights.

It may well be that this increase in local, intranational, and intraregional violence and disorganization will constitute a major hazard to the commitment to law which will be necessary for the maintenance of a warless world. Just as many people rejoiced because Mussolini made the trains run on time, so a demand for local order may run counter to the demand for world order.

The abolition of the use of armed force will by no means lead to the abolition of other types of competition and conflict or attempts to resolve these through the application of various kinds of pressure. This prospect often is viewed simply as the reappearance of the old Adam—the expression of hostility and aggression in new, substitute forms. However, such conflicts are better viewed as the formal concomitants of whatever institutional arrangements in regard to trade, migration, recruitment and proselytizing, the use of natural resources, and the world-wide management of the world-relevant environment—the atmosphere, outer space, the deep seas—which we succeed in establishing. Here again, conflict does not represent some new outbreak of innate hostility which must find expression. Rather, it represents the existence of social institutions and various kinds of social situations which, because of their style, generate opposition and aggression against opponents instead of generating cooperation.

Furthermore, unless continuous precautions are taken, men in one part of the world may seek to alter the common environment without regard for the rest of the planet's people. The absence of military force may also tempt the enterprising into a subtler warfare of control of the minds and souls of their fellow men. New opportunities provided by the application of science—

new drugs, subliminal television, the infrared posteffect camera
—all such things as these will provide new temptations to exploit other men within one nation and between nations. Certain
new discoveries, especially those which make it possible to preserve life in grossly distorted or deteriorating forms, present
moral problems that have barely been glimpsed by the ingenious
constructors of utopias and counterutopias.

In a warless world a great mass of unsolved problems will suddenly stand out in high relief. Old and new, they represent a
challenge and a guarantee that men will not be able to sink
into overdomestication and dull security. On the contrary, it is
the threat of nuclear catastrophe and annihilation which is today
producing apathy and withdrawal. In wartime people breed heed-
lessly; under nuclear threat they are walling themselves into
small suburban refuges against dread and despair. Only a restored faith in the future, a renewed sense of continuity can give
men the strength and the will to commit themselves to the hard
work of making a viable world community.

The development of nation-states with enormous urban populations underwrote science and, having made modern warfare
possible, in the end made it intolerable. At the same time, men
were further and further removed from those qualities of strength
and skill and endurance which for millennia had stood them in
good stead. Nevertheless, however much the small boy was re-
buked for fighting and for cruelty, however much he was en-
joined to cooperate with his classmates, to drive carefully, to
keep his feet dry, however much he was hemmed in and made to
sit still, the mere knowledge that he might one day be called on
to expend every ounce of his physical strength and skill and
even lay down his life for his country, gave some symbolic support to his masculinity. For many men this possibility served
in some measure as a surrogate for hardships and dangers that
were never faced; the dangers of the jungle and the sea and the
windy heights of mountains; wild beasts; hunger and thirst; and
the challenge of his own equals, unflinchingly faced, man to
man. The extraordinary bravery of city-bred, poorly exercised,
inexpert draft armies testifies to the partial effectiveness of this
surrogate.

In a warless world, this will be gone. It will be necessary then to give all boys, healthier and more robustly grown than any earlier generation, new ways and much greater chances to test their mettle and the extent to which they can expect their bodies to stand up to trials of strength, skill, poise, and personal danger. It will be necessary, in effect, to establish a different kind of physical life. In taking away war, which had been transformed into wholesale annihilation for which men could only wait passively, we may, indeed we must, give human beings a much closer relationship to their own bodies.

As long as man's need to contend with and match his strength against his fellow men was epitomized by his behavior in war, we saw it majorly as based on hostility. Detached from exploitation in warfare and given freer play, we can see this contending behavior for what it actually is: a measure of and a symbol for a young male's delight in growth. What we need most are political equivalents for the functions which war has served in promoting the interests of human groups and man's pride in their relationships to a group of their fellow men. Given these, then, man's psychological need to display skill and courage, to protect and contend for all he values and loves can be channeled in new directions. Free from the threat of war, exploration of outer space and the depth of the seas awaits his efforts.

# XII

## The spiritual effect of warlessness

BY WILLIAM ERNEST HOCKING

Philosopher and educator, author of
*The Coming World Civilization* and
*Strength of Men and Nations: A Message to
the USA vis-à-vis the USSR*

The shadow which the bare possibility of nuclear war casts over the human spirit is not solely the shadow of measureless calamity. Is is that; but it is also a shadow over human self-respect, and over the entire scope of human faith.

Over human self-respect: Because we feel that at the summit of the technical achievements of our proud civilization we have reached a point in some respect lower than its beginning. In dealing with radical contests of interest, purpose, and belief—contests inseparable from human aspiration and experiment—we have conceived and are prepared to use a type of warfare which releases over human centers forces indiscriminate in their action —forces vast, mindless, merciless, uncontrollable when released —in complete reversal of the direction of advance hitherto in the arts of war.

Over human faith in its entire scope: I am speaking of all faith, including that "animal faith" of which Santayana writes, and the unformulated faith men live by, that elemental confidence, living spontaneously in the future, attending every natural impulse to act. Nuclear war confronts faith in this broad sense with a total negation, since for extended human groups the entire future would in an instant be obliterated. This negation holds whether or not the group involved is our own: it is our conception of human destiny that is at stake. For consider:

The infant creature of whatever species faces a world literally unknown, in which—without any prior certification of success—it has to act: a commitment to action-on-impulse is a condition of any life whatever. A sense of risk is a later phase of awareness. What the opening life assumes is that its launch-out will be responded to: "If I take wing, I'll be sustained; what else is the world there for?" It is only the maturing creature that undertakes to chart its future and assess risks. And even so, *faith that the future can be shaped* remains the core of action, and especially of human action: the provision for "a calculable future" remains the basis of all orderly society. But *what if there were no future?*

Time indeed cannot stop; but human continuities can be canceled—the concrete future. And if there is no concrete future, to what extent can the present moment of life hold its meaning?

As in space, we live habitually in a world room without limit, galaxies receding ad infinitum, so in time, we inhabit a present moment which is "the conflux of two eternities," past and future. And quite spontaneously we estimate the meaning of this here-and-now in terms of what sense, what *telos,* what accomplishment we feel or fancy for the whole world process into futurity. Of course, if our present moment has no worth, then the totality of such moments can have none; but also, if the whole is empty of sense, the momentary items lose their meaning. Meaning, I say, runs from the whole to the part, and if there is no whole to which the part can contribute, the edifice of meaning collapses. Pleasures remain; but *happiness,* as implying endless vistas and a sense of at-homeness and participation in the universe—happiness is no longer possible. It is this loss of horizon, and of personal destiny and function, contributing to a total world achievement, that darkens the world to which nuclear war is admitted. How has this darkening occurred?

Not by argument. It has occurred silently, and over a considerable time, as a quiet implication of our concentrated activities: first, in tracing the secrets and histories of the physical energies of the world, as the best-documented bit of "reality" we can discover; second, in applying these discoveries to the special political impasse of our times, resulting in the invention of a particular kind of war. We have hardly noticed that the type of war thus resulting is *definitely not war* in any traditional sense; nor that its use—and we Americans have made one use of it— carries a confession, eloquent beyond words, that we no longer subscribe to certain "self-evident truths" on which we still imagine our special type of democracy to be founded: purely by implication the "unalienable right" to life of the ordinary civilian is completely canceled.

Traditional war is an institution with its definite internal organization: it is a corporate operation to enforce a national purpose in which citizens may be assumed to share, and may thus rightly be called on to serve. The group thus assembled is held together by a unanimity of purpose transcending the individual's life purpose, but *including it*. It is in risking his own life for the national purpose that the soldier achieves a temporary suspension of the law against killing; but prior to that, war itself implies a suspension of the fundamental rule of all morality: treat persons as persons, never as things. War consists in treating the enemy as a thing, a physical obstacle, and as such not to be reasoned with, conversed with, appealed to as a being capable of reason, but to be blasted out of the way. When traditional war begins, conversation with the enemy stops; but it remains possible for conversation to be resumed, so long as a conversable fragment of the enemy survives. But the type of warfare now attained is not carried on between groups of warriors animated by a common will to serve the cause at whatever cost: it is not concerned with survivors. The target has become not a distinct purposive enemy, but a group of communities going about everyday concerns, to be visited by an instant annihilating roar. Persons no longer count: men, women, children, with their petty local interests, loves, ambitions, . . . become irrelevant bits of litter: only one reality is pertinent, namely, $e = mc^2$. As William Barrett has put it, man is now "free to deal with the world in all its brute objectivity."

Such "war," Barrett says, is no longer war, but an engineering operation which we now know how to manage. It calls for precise instrumentation, information, and operative skill; but for no regimentation, no flags, no marching, no songs, no ritual . . . and not always for the personal courage of the operator. Its main disadvantage is that the operation could be turned on ourselves, and that, too, would not be war. For war in its traditional sense —with all its treatment of persons as things—was intended to be a sort of argument, destined to end in a resumed conversation, called "peace." The new war could not even end in a graveyard, as in Kant's bitter image of "perpetual peace." For there could be no graves, and—except for peripheral accident—no remains to put into them—*spurlos verbrannt*. Images of a "resurrection of the body" lose all pertinent factual contact.

We of the United States have never attempted a war on the nuclear pattern, though at enormous cost we continue to equip ourselves for instant action. But we have already used the technique to terminate a conventional war. In so doing we have saved a possible million of hypothetical lives by blotting out a few hundred thousand actual lives, among them those of the children whose burning so haunted the sleep of Major Eatherly. We have thus supplied the world with an exhibit of the nature of nuclear war, and ourselves with a specimen of its repercussions —both amply sufficient.

And thus, with our help, the shadow cast over the human spirit has become substantial, and we can now discern its nature:

When human life and its meaning can be thus abruptly broken off, something must happen to that *picture of futurity* which attends all human action, as the field of its fulfilled meaning. Here the shadow enters to denounce any hopeful forecast of the destiny of our deeds as entering into the total meaning of the world process: it is precisely this wholeness that must be dismissed. And while world religions partly escape this threat, occupying themselves less with kingdoms of God on earth than with other-worldly prospects, these other-worldly visions are not immune to the judgments of reality implied by the working charts of the military, for whom the master reality is physical energy. Religion per se becomes quietly suspect of total irrelevance.

Malleable minds—and especially youthful minds—are thus driven to estimates of the dominant world forces closely akin to those of our planetary neighbors who subscribe to something called dialectical materialism (not quite as brittle as it sounds!). For the Institutes of Philosophy in Moscow are now driven by the advance of physics (which plays no political favorites) to accept the translation of "materialism" into "energism"; and further, in order to sustain the ethical activism desired in a Socialist society, "matter," they now say, must be considered "autodynamic." There is thus, I venture to say, little practical difference between the two materialisms that profess themselves mortal opponents: each of them placing its trust in nuclear-weapon superiority, or response-ability.

It is in this atmosphere that the youth of our Western lands are moving toward maturity. For them, faith in any total meaning of the world process has become a dubious placebo. What, then, must become of their faith in *their own* total meaning, or in any type of obligation built into the nature of things, including those sensitive obligations to truth which have built this very noble world of the physical sciences? It is the general acceptance by nations presumably at the peak of those moral achievements represented by civilized law-observance and by the arts and letters as well as the sciences—it is, I say, the *general acceptance* of this type of war as usable *in extremis,* that constitutes for our youth the chief silent repudiation of its professed faiths, including the belief that this universe as a whole has a meaning.

And the *greatest effect on the human spirit* of an achieved warless world would be the *lifting of this shadow,* especially from the spirit of youth. The effect would be the more pronounced if the achievement were itself brought about *by measures of mind and moral conviction,* rather than by a stalemate in the field of military prowess. Let me, then, turn to the affirmative inquiry: By what mental and moral measures can we achieve a world order in which contest—the life of all important advance—can take place without war?

## Moral bases for contest without war

The actual arrival of the nuclear-war threat had its apparent justification. The continuing argument in its favor is its swift decisiveness: if there is to be war at all, no rational power can neglect the most efficient tools of defence. And so long as public power on a limited planet contains an ingrained bent to expansion, encouraged perhaps by some obsession of a world mission not shared by all others, dissenting powers can hardly choose less than the most formidable deterrent.

If then, the aggressor—unreasonably ambitious or inspired— is equally equipped with nuclear weapons, the outlook for humanity is indeed dark. For to divest one's nation of maximal deterrent power is an open invitation to the smile on the face of the tiger; whereas to retain that deterrent is to invite the ultimate catastrophe. The Cuba quarantine episode presented a case of just this hostile confrontation of the two leading nuclear powers; and its fortunate denouement has been variously interpreted. To my mind it illustrates the most hopeful factor in the structure of a warless world, namely the *inner deterrent* to war, which has strangely passed unrecognized. For note:

The decision of Khrushchev to withdraw was a decision compelled not primarily by the nuclear power of the United States but by a clear inhibition in the mind of the Soviet leader; not only was the Russian public rootedly averse to war, but the simplest human common sense forbade the carnage. That this *inner deterrence* was mutual is indicated by the exchange of notes between the two leaders, in which the phrase—strange as between official enemies—the phrase "you and I" *occurs in both.* This inner deterrence illustrates the main principle of peaceful coexistence, namely, that *underlying every fundamental contest, there must be a fundamental agreement.* The future of mankind depends largely on the general recognition of this simple thesis: that *every dispute has its presuppositions* on which the contending parties necessarily agree, if only as to the value of the objectives claimed by each. If war of any kind is to be dismissed, then—since disputes among men and nations are a constant crop from lively foreign policies—the art of finding the necessary common ground becomes a primary essential—no, *the* primary essential.

On one of these matters it is possible even now to establish firm common ground, and this perhaps the most apparently threatening: the aim of "world conquest" as the avowed goal and necessary terminus of the dialectic of history in the Marx-Lenin tradition. A necessary victory embodied in the historical process, whether expounded by Marx or by Hegel, is the destiny of every valid ideal as long as humanity strives for what it sees as "the good." We democrats believe with Hegel in the world conquest of democracy: The whole burden of history for Hegel is embedded in nine words: *one* is free; *some* are free; *all* are free. Hegel and Marx are at opposite poles: but their strife presupposes one fundamental agreement—"truth is mighty and must prevail." *No world conquest by force or fraud is seriously contemplated by any actual power;* and the actual strife of ideologies, taking a competitive form, implies not only the concern of each competitor for the continued existence of the other (the conquest of either by the other would destroy the competition), but also for the fair chance of each to develop its own type of social structure. Under such circumstances the competition becomes part of the education of mankind, whose lessons are read—currently by all interested persons—but officially by whatever body represents the united nations. The vicious circle which sustains the actual Cold War is thus broken: A must destroy B, because B is committed to destroy A; and B is committed to destroy A because A is vowed to destroy B. When it appears that each premise is false, the circle disappears; and the sense of the Cold War vanishes.

In this inquiry there emerges another moral interest which contributes to the spirit of the warless world, namely, the *interest in variety*. The coexistence of opposing ideologies during the period of experimentation opens the picture of a closure of the contest, as with every good game, in the victory of one party and the defeat of the other. But difference is not always and necessarily an opposition between right and wrong; it may be a valued aspect of the rich possibilities of human nature.

It is true that a warless world implies a world agreed on certain principles of public order, the primary outlines of an international code of law. But it is not true that as a consequence the legal structure of all free states will be identical, whether in the institutions of the family, or of property, or of contract, or of torts. In 1930, there was published a new Civil Code for Nationalist

China. In his Preface to the English version of the first volume of the Code, the editor notes that this work "follows in its theoretical positions the principles which the modern juridical science is spreading steadily all over the world, and which are tending to constitute a sort of universal common law, and to remove the discrepancies due to the dissimilarities of the various national legislations. . . ." He then points out that China is unable to follow this trend in two significant fields, the law of real property and the law of the family. Here local tradition and usage mark out a unique historical achievement, having its own contribution to a universal judgment of the meaning of law.

This is indicative of one character of law which calls for more general recognition on a more anthropological basis than that of Savigny: its rootage in local custom and history. Even the most primary principles of right, such as the maxims of Ulpian in the *Digest—honeste vivere, neminem laedere, cuique suum tribuere* —take various shapes in different social orders. When Dean Pound in his recent Mooers Lecture sought a "foundation for jurisprudence" he found himself unwilling to commit himself to any fixed formula. The common law of England and most of the United States could for the most part be defined as the *coinage of custom;* folkways worked out by experience in societies which, in Royce's phrase, are "communities of memory and of hope." There must indeed be general principles of common human decency, whereby travelers and traders can pass from state to state and find reasonable conditions of intercourse; hence the durability of early maritime and commercial law; but the individual quality of the nation remains one of the great interests of travel as well as one of the moral assets of the race. We may therefore consider *the nation* as an individual *experiment in lawmaking,* so that the diversities of the laws—far exceeding those of Montesquieu's *Esprit des Lois*—constitute one of the treasures which the world would be deeply reluctant to lose in a mechanical uniformity. While this variousness of national type constitutes one of the chief obstacles to the successful codification of international law, a developed *appreciation of difference* promises to be a major help to the realization of a warless world.

We can realize world unity in the proposal that there is an

absolute right in which all humanity agrees, while agreeing that
the formulation of that absolute principle is subject to wide and
characteristic differences of opinion. We are in no sense committed to a boundless and formless relativity.

## The case of conventional war

It is not sufficient to dismiss nuclear war. The warless world,
still having its occasions of strife over unsolved problems of
justice, national interest, and arbitrary boundaries, must find its
way to solutions not involving the mobilization of opposing
armies whose instruments will drift toward the mass-destructive
type.

The problem remains with us, because if solutions cannot be
found by reason, the alternative appears to be a solution determined by that *power, inseparable from human government,
which expresses the united resolve of the nation.* The "national
interest," as a term reserved in usual treaties of arbitration, represents a factor of *will,* commonly arbitrary, into which a nation
puts its "honor," as a sign of decision—irrational in the sense of
not being deducible from generally accepted principles. The accidents of geography cannot be derived from principles of justice:
does Switzerland deserve a seacoast? Has Russia a right to access
to the Mediterranean? Has the United States a manifest destiny
to include California? Has Nepal, perched high in the Himalayas,
with no natural access to great centers, a right to any independent
statehood whatever, with its keep-off demands upon its natural
neighbors?

The radical difference between domestic law and international
law is this: for domestic law the units are human individuals finished by nature on a pattern having a generic uniformity,
whereas for world law the units—the nations—have *no natural
biology.* No one knows when or whether they are finished, nor
even when they are fully born. Nor have they any natural life
span, any natural death, any indication from nature when they
should merge, separate, divide as human organisms cannot do,
and as nation-states have frequently found desirable or necessary. A federal union might find its analogy in some coral colonies, but more accurately in some monster composed of fifty

Siamese twins; but the "rights" of the units could hardly be inferred from analogue. At any rate, the variety of size and capacity and cultural productivity and age and promise among nations renders spurious any attempt to make *equality* a guide to justice. There is a generic comradeship among states that have demonstrated a capacity for intelligent lawmaking and "good government"; but equality, as a quantitative ideal, even among men in society, is all too often the bitch goddess of envy: it bears on the rights of nations only to the extent of indicating the complement of physiological functions of a viable political organism. Aside from this, if our hope of a warless world is based on the faith that issues between nations can be determined by justice, we must admit that we have as yet *no substantial guide to what justice is among nation-states*. It is all the more important to emphasize the value of variety of which we have spoken, and the coming unity of a world civilization to which such minor odd corners of the world as Palestine or Athens or the Nejd or Budh Gaya in its day may make the decisive contributions too well hidden from the noisy atmosphere of the physically greater nations.

The *right to exist as a nation-state* is the one right from which other rights—rights to the necessary conditions of fruitful existence—may follow. But that original right to exist must be held in reserve, as depending not on any political *cogito ergo sum,* "Here I am, respect me and give me the necessities of life," but on the consensus of states representing the existing world civilization, expressed through the acts of "recognition," as acts of hope, justified only by subsequent fertility, or, let me say, creativity.

To what extent, then, can this world community dispense with conventional war?

The individual state, being a creature of a deed of trust on the part of the recognizing states, has a duty of honor to justify their trust. But, since each national life has its own unique conditions, it must be its own judge as to what is necessary to its creative productivity. India and China may arbitrarily "set their honor" on a fragment of territory in Ladakh. Then the would-be warless world finds itself calling for arms and aid.

We have no right to be discouraged by these reversals; they indicate simply that the unity of mankind, already a voice of hope and admonition, has not yet become a voice of paternal love and authority, able to deal with unique claims as *unique and individual* for the sake of the truly spiritual unity of a creative whole. The words of Camus are still valid: it is the artist who holds the secret of a vital peace, "when the collective passions of mankind put the fate of the whole world at stake"—for it is the voice of faith and feeling rather than the voice of law to which armed power will one day listen, as the completer voice of its own deeper will.

Until there is such a voice, heard by a unanimous membership of the nations qualified not simply as peace-loving (what nation will not assert its share in this sentiment?) but as already appreciating and contributing to the advance of world civilization, we must move deeper into the moral recesses of that will to war which still, from time to time, betrays the human spirit.

In dismissing war *tout court,* we are aware of making a breach with history. There is a nagging query to which we are bound to lend a passing ear. Does the spirit of man lose—if war is gone— a certain challenge which, until now, has been a measure of its own greatness?

When the Socrates of Plato speaks of virtue, his first mention is of courage, "the spirited faculty." The Greek gymnasium was a preparation for the field, and Socrates himself was distinguished as a soldier. Throughout Western history, the drilling of youth in the perspective of a possible clash of arms has been an ingredient of education. And through our versions of history, the glory of the great men of war resounds: the great wrong of the aggressor measures the great right of our resistance and his defeat. Shall we now lose that dimension?

Our own psychological insights have something to say. We are not born pugnacious; but "pugnacity" is in the background, a latent, subconscious tendency, with its own reserve store of energy waiting to reinforce a positive impulse meeting resistance. The resolute response of purpose to a grasping or malicious offence is part of our Darwinian fitness to survive (and I have known mothers who anxiously waited for signs that their infant sons had within themselves a spring of resentment against torment from other infant sons); but by the same sign it is also part of our mental and moral completeness. Response to an inflicted pain should distinguish factually and morally between the accidental and the intended!

This organic readiness to resist implies that combat is an expectable part of experience. And as in our own natures, so in our communities common foresight makes normal provision for the abnormal possibilities. And our young manhood adjusts itself (not without friction) to these demands of political prudence: time out for military training. Knowing deeply the capacity for ill-will within itself it accepts the outer contingency, with a mixture of incredulity and accepted enlightenment. In his depths, the male youth knows that there is a time for facing "the facts of life," a phrase quite as pertinent to the dawning life of combat as to the dawning life of sex.

What is to happen, then, in the deeps of our nature, to the higher moments of our pugnacity, recognizing as one of the invisible realities of the environment a type of will whose tendency is to treat humanity other than itself as *a means to its own ends,* definitely not as an end in itself. The offender is, of course, making a metaphysical mistake; and the simplest sign of resentment may be sufficient to remind him that "I, too, am a person"; or, in Confucius's terms, "the returning of good for evil that goodness may be created" may not only correct him but alter his motivation. But when the issue appears on the corporate or national level, the immediate personal reaction has to be sublimated into a community response into which personal responses must be regimented. It is less easy to rectify a corporate aggressor than a personal foe. Shall we find ways to peace which call for no devoted enlistment in the public resistance? Are we then ready with what William James called a "moral equivalent of war," to steel with some systematic severities our own acceptance of pain and risk, lest we fall into a state of which he commented "Fie upon such a cattle-yard of a planet!"? What is that potential element of human dignity in the soldier for which—if we succeed in putting war behind us—we may still require a moral equivalent?

It is inadequate to think of this matter—or of any matter involving the depth psychology of human beings on an historic scale—in terms of generalities. Each of us is inclined to think of it in terms of some family background, perhaps of the Civil War, unless his experience has touched one or more of the recent world wars. Let me speak briefly of such a personal experience.

Military camps everywhere and always are highly artificial communities, in their nature an abstraction from normal community life. One's tent mate becomes an important factor in one's thinking and being; but my temporary "buddy" at Plattsburg in 1916 was an unusual gift of Providence. We were all volunteers, civilians for the most part who considered that the United States ought to prepare for taking part in the war in Europe. But James Norman Hall was no novice. He had deliberately inserted himself, from the beginning of the war, first into active preparation terminating at Aldershot, and then into the midst of the fierce fighting in Flanders.

He was an Iowa boy, a graduate of Grinnell College in 1914, a "woodshed poet" by disposition. He had been spending the summer in England, when war broke out and England prepared to assist France and Belgium against the German attack. As an American he was under no call to enlist—the British recruiting stations raised all the relevant difficulties—but he felt that the German breach of Europe's long-standing peace was no local concern: it was the Western world order that must react. He trained several months in the artillery, then served in a machine-gun squad in Flanders. When he was mustered out toward the end of 1915, and came home on account of his father's illness, he was the only survivor of his squad. He entered the Plattsburg Civilian Training Camp, not to learn the arts of war, but to explore what the United States was doing to prepare for our part in the deepening conflict. He was naturally a marked man, and was offered a major's rank if he would stay and share in the staff work of the camp. But he had other plans: he was bound to return to the front. And further, he had recognized that this war would involve, for the first time in history, reconnaissance by airplane. An American flying unit was being assembled in France, the Lafayette Flying Squadron: Hall joined it, and when he went again to the French front I lost sight of him for a time.

In the spring of 1917, our news carried the report that Norman Hall had been shot down over the German lines, and was presumably killed. During that summer, I had an assignment at the British and French fronts which gave me an occasion to be in Paris, where, on a bank register, I happened to see the name of Norman Hall. Nothing else was important: I found him at Hotel Normandy, and we had a day together. He had indeed been shot down. His reconnaissance team had had a program of flight over the German lines and a well-defined rendezvous for return. One day, spying a group of planes he took for his own, he steered to them, but they were German. They opened fire; his plane was hit and he was shot through the shoulder. "I dimly realized that unless I could bring the two levers together it was the end; I made the effort, and blanked out. Don't know how I landed." But it was within the French lines, and involved a long period in a French hospital before transfer to an American hospital at Neuilly.

He was still far from fit. On a foot trip with me to *la Cité* he had twice to sit down and rest; he was due next day in camp for retraining, hoping to be assigned to the region of Verdun-sur-Meuse, scene of the most obstinate fighting of the war, and the most costly in terms of men. (Joffre had been replaced by Pétain after an unexampled mutiny of units driven too often to a futile assault, on a mistaken tactic of repeated attack in a "War of Attrition"; though of its magnificent determination Larousse remarks that it *émerveilla l'univers!*) Here Hall concluded his war service, and returned home, to become a writer.

But Hall was no lover of war, and no seeker for adventure for adventure's sake. The life in the Escadrille Lafayette filled him with depression; early experiments in flying were full of tragedy: "We had so often to go and clean up a mess that had been a comrade." But he had also come to feel, in the postwar cities of Europe and America, a failure to examine the causes of war and to avoid its repetition; men "returned to the old greeds and hatreds"; if this is "civilization," it is less than worthy the name.

This feeling was a factor in his later choice (with Nordhoff) of Tahiti as a home.

What was the central motive impelling him into war? Patriotic he was; but it was not patriotism as a passion for serving one's own country that inspired his major decisions. He *had to explore the breakdown of peace in order to judge the structure of normal living;* he was trying to build, through harsh experience, the mental image of a world more genuine, more humane, more universal in sympathy and understanding. As a predestined writer, he must *know* life in its depths and heights. He never ceased to *think* over the causes and cures of the war tragedy: of his time in the hospital he said to me, "It had one great advantage, I had *time to think;* that's what we need!"

Hall has described both his early feelings about enlistment in the war, and his later judgments of disillusion, in his book *My Island Home.* The spirit of England in the fall of 1914 he described with the incredible word "joy"—"a kind of deep, solemn, sacred joy" expressed in the words of Rupert Brooke:

> Now God be thanked who matched us with His hour,
> And caught our youth, and wakened us from sleeping,
> With hand made sure, clear eye, and sharpened power,
> To turn, as sleepers into cleanness leaping, . . .
> Leave the sick hearts that honour could not move, . . . .

Hall then remarked on the vast change in men's feeling concerning war even before the close of World War I—it had become inconceivable that a poet could speak of "young men, with the best of life before them, and each one eager to make the most of it, as 'sleepers into cleanness leaping'—into the horror, shame, and degradation of war." As for himself, "I was cured of whatever illusions I may have had as to war being a noble adventure, but this was not till later."

And in spite of his bitter retrospect on war *per se,* there was— I must believe—an element of nobility in his commitment to sharing the most desperate phases of human experience in the mission—which is an all-human mission—of understanding the lot of man in a universe which contains tragedy.

I try to find a single term for Hall's spirit as a soldier, a spirit for which one could wish a "moral equivalent": it is, in a phrase, a *search for reality in experience,* a need to experience the worst in order to realize the cost of the best. As a responsible member of the race, he could not be content with an accidentally sheltered good fortune.

Royce had a phrase for it which came near the target; "loyalty to a cause" seemed to him the highest virtue of man.

But nearer still is the word of Alfred de Vigny in *La Canne de Jonc* (and de Vigny has been through the storm of revolution). His word is "honor," and he describes his meaning in these lines:

> It is a virtue entirely human . . .
> a sentiment born with us, independent of times and places,
> and even of the religions,
> a sentiment proud, inflexible, an instinct of incomparable
>     beauty. . . .
> It is the *faith of HONOR*.

The term "honor" carries with it a self-defined and self-enforced obligation, one—like the "debt of honor"—that cannot be compelled by either law or usage; at its height, an unwritten obligation of membership in the human race, the duty of knowing what it is to be a man, and of paying the full cost, which no one has prescribed.

With this understanding, we can see that the banishing of war —if the objects sought by war could be otherwise attained— would banish nothing of honor, nor of loyalty, nor of courage. We have no need to cherish war in order to cherish the greatness that war has so often elicited in men. The moral equivalent of war lies in the spiritual essence of a man's honor, carrying him into whatever risk, adventure, sacrifice, suffering may be involved in fulfilling the task prescribed by his destiny.

It remains true that the military camp occupies a place in the education of men for which there is as yet no adequate substitute. There is a time for specific service of the community in its physical aspects, *a regimented and compulsory service,* under officers who must be obeyed—officers who know their job thoroughly, maintain discipline, and share the hardship they require for their men. There is a time for the masculine community, for a monasticism accepted and honestly observed, for *a man's judgment of a man,* not to be evaded by easy resort to feminine acceptance—the fatal blemish of coeducational college life. And there are many public tasks which such a camp can fitly undertake, as in clearing mountain trails, mending broken levees, building dams . . . the work of an intentionally abstract community dedicated to corporate hardship at the moving frontier of a nation's life, and enjoying a type of fellowship for which human experience has no equivalent.

Human history finds its most well-marked segments at the points of man's growing control of physical forces, the domestication of animals, the use of tools, the invention of gunpowder, the engine, the "tele"-one-thing-and-another, the release of nuclear energy. War has its epochs based on these physical periods. In each of these periods, the increasing phenomenon of mass murder has called forth increasing revolt against war itself: the scale of tragedy now robs war of the dignity of an accepted sacrifice —the word "tragedy," having its own dignity, becomes impertinent. But this, its final phase, throws into stark relief the element of contradiction which attends war per se at any period, and animates the spiritual relief when war, as now, commits suicide.

At all stages, as I have pointed out, war treats human beings as things, not as persons. Yet it depends for its effect on their *continuing personality:* its intention is not to exterminate but to impose change upon their wills: The population behind the army is to survive, with an enforced change of condition and judgment. The contradiction in war-making begins here, with the manifest absurdity in the assumption that a change of thought, of belief, of ideology can be *imposed by force.* It is the chronic illusion of political power that it can compel belief: the explicit repudiation of this deceit would constitute an epoch of liberation for the spirit of man.

This inner conflict—inherent in war—lends to all the dealings of war a flavor of lawlessness: it is not only killing that becomes the order of things—the "all's fair" includes the lie, the spying, the cover story for the public, the highly "classified" information, while "truth in the news" remains the professed practice, the reason of state, and everywhere the license for cruelty. Even in the reported sacred wars of the chosen people, one is startled at the treatment proposed for the Amalekites, or for the Babylonians in view of their guilt in the Captivity: "In that day shall thy babes be taken and dashed against the stones. . . ." A fit prelude to modern history as exemplified—let us say—in what we have done to inhabitants of our great southwest in the name of "manifest destiny." In the University of Tokyo there was formerly (and possibly still is) a Hepburn Professorship of American Constitutional Law. A former incumbent of that chair, Professor Yasaka Takagi, told me that he enjoyed transmitting these ideas of law to Japanese youth, except when it came to the Mexican War. And he added that his difficulty was not solely with the trumped-up pretexts on which that war was fought, but as much with the fact that, little as he could approve the means, he felt compelled to approve the result: he would not now wish California a province of Mexico. War has at times appeared as a disgraceful means to a justified end, a means which in a degree poisons the satisfaction in the end, and adds to our relief at the repudiation of war.

And within the texture of the fighting unit itself—not to mention the conflicts of moral judgment attending the off-duty conduct of enlisted men irked by the routine, the artificial duplicity in relations with the camp-following circle, and the incomplete rapport with official interpretations of a campaign's purpose— how often, or rather how chronically, the enlisted man's private sense of *honor* has to struggle against the duties imposed by military obedience (as in Henry Denker's play, *The Hook*). There are, I believe, not a few Americans for whom the U2 episode, which broke up the Paris Conference of May, 1960, was a moral disaster in respect to their esteem for the strict probity of high official direction.

In a warless world, one great relief for the human spirit must be a final farewell to the appalling casuistry involved on the part of officialdom in maintaining faith with the public, and on the part of the public in maintaining faith in the complete justice and cleanliness of a "just war"—a phrase which we must hope finally to banish.

The effect of a warless world on the spirit of man, at its core, will not be primarily the negative reliefs—the lifting of the cloud of nuclear war over the total meaning of life, the escape from the inner contradictions of all human war-making, from the "shame, horror, and degradation" of war. It will be a joy of discovery, a new experience of power.

For man is spiritually free only when he shares in the power which rules the cosmos, taking part in the process of creation. And the warless world will require a certain achievement of unanimity in the will to banish an intolerable curse; and the achievement of that unanimity will itself be an act—certainly not of physical power—but of a power to change human motivation.

Man's will, at its center, is a *will to power* in a sense not contemplated by Hobbes or Nietzsche. It is a rejection of futility, an assumption of command over some portion of future happening, *making occur* what ought to occur, bringing the creativity of the artist to supplement the regulative work of the lawmaker, giving effect to that *inner deterrent* which we found as a will-to-peace at the kernel of the obdurate war-maker.

For an act of creative power—a power not *over* others but *for* others, and a power first over *ideas* before being a power over *actions*—the way is cleared by the now evident general repudiation—Mao Tse-tung still remaining enigmatic—of mass destruction as a means of survival, rendering obsolete that consultation of the witches called cybernetics which instructs us as to the comparative survival values of the various extant civilizations after the losses of $x$ or $y$ hundred million members.

With this relief, we are still left with unresolved problems of right and justice, and the temptation of a powerful opponent to take decisions into his own hand—the renewal of war-making after war-rejection cannot be excluded; and the disposition would reappear for speculation as to the trustworthiness of our opponent, with furtive explorations as to his motivation. This residual timidity and passivity wholly neglects the supreme moral capacity of the human spirit, the *capacity to create in an opponent the temper we can trust.*

It is this capacity which marks the whole sense of "resist not evil" as an improvement on "an eye for an eye": the idea of the "go with him twain" is not that of quiescent submission to outrage; it is that of *altering the temper* of the enemy. It is the intent of Camus' Rebel who in presence of a demand which is unjust and at the risk of his life, refuses to obey, not because he is averse to the action, but because the Master at heart knows it wrong: the Rebel, assured of this, takes the step that creates solidarity. This great conception of Camus is precisely pertinent to the world problem of today. It involved an act of faith, but not the softheaded acquiescence of dull amiability—it is faith in a well-thought-out plan of co-existence, and a willingness to risk the consecutive stages of disarmament, on the basis of *an achieved certitude,* as to the fundamental motivation of the opponent, a well-created *will to partnership* in the development of a workable world order.

In its program, it would recognize that the "enemy" is the most important member to include in a new world order, based on that recognized *necessary agreement* which we found as the presupposition of all definable contests, to which a community of widely—and valuably—differing nations is liable. The problems of such a community may not be less formidable than the problems of an obsolete Cold War; but they are problems faced with a new joy, a joy as deep, solemn, and sacred as that with which Rupert Brooke rose to the summons of the First World War— the joy of *sharing in the process of creation,* with the total hierarchy of creative powers of that reality in which we live and move have our being.

# XIII

## Proposals for study and action

BY JAMES J. WADSWORTH

Former United States Ambassador to
the United Nations and disarmament negotiator.

We have seen in the preceding chapters that, optimists though
they are, our scholars and experts recognize the almost fantastic
difficulties that lie between today's tensions and a warless world.
They would not have anyone believe that a wave of the wand can
bring about all the basic changes that such a world will demand,
even before we embark on the uncharted course of changes that
are needed once we have achieved such a world. Truly, it is
brought home to all of us that homo sapiens and his institutions
still have a long and weary way to go before they see the millennium.

One is all the more impressed, therefore, that jurists, profes-
sors, government ministers, historians, and research directors,
among others, far from being appalled by the road blocks which
stand athwart the ways to peace, are able quietly to assume that
the roads are traversable and that the requisite planning and
thinking can be done without serious harm to anyone's "way of
life." In this book there is no fanaticism, nor any bland attitude
of sweeping under the rug anything that cannot readily be solved.
Here is the inquiring mind, searching the probabilities and con-
cluding that they exist for us if only we desire them enough.

In recognizing the possibilities, the authors have also recognized the difficulties and have handed them to us for study and
identification and tactical operation. These difficulties are divided
roughly into six parts: political, economic, military, educational

and informational, sociological, and legal. After studying the chapters, the reader becomes convinced that the changes growing out of the *realization* of the assumptions handed the various authors are manageable, at least for the most part. On the other hand, I find myself seriously concerned with the preparations that are needed *before* the assumptions can be validated. In order to arrive at G & CD Day,* when all the machinery described and arguments adduced in the foregoing chapters can be put into operation, what needs to be done?

There is little value in dissecting each of the preceding chapters in turn in order to point out the obvious questions which they pose. This might seem critical, which would be untenable, or it might seem hair-splitting, which should be avoided. I shall, therefore, take up the six major divisions just mentioned and discuss them in the context of what questions must be solved in order to bring about the conditions which the earlier chapters assumed.

## Political possibilities

First of all, we need to recognize the existence and the demands of change, as described so well in the chapters written by Walter Millis, Arnold Toynbee, and Arthur Larson. We must anticipate the political developments that must take place, and we must plan for channeling the forces of change into the stream beds which lead logically to our warless world. This means that through diplomacy, education, and public information we must work for the official and public acceptance of certain political goals. Nations may prefer various methods of arriving at these goals, in accordance with their traditions, experience, present form of government, and present position vis-à-vis the rest of the world. It is doubtful, in fact, that identical paths will be followed by any two nations.

It will be necessary, therefore, to initiate studies on a unilateral basis as to the best and least dislocating methods of arriving at a political posture which in most cases will demand deep and broad adjustments for achievement. The posture necessary for a successful G & CD Day includes a whole series of "willingnesses" which may not exist in nations today—willingness:

* General and Complete Disarmament Day.

To abide by an international set of rules promulgated by an international body and enforced by an international police force;

To accept International Court of Justice jurisdiction, and to see that jurisdiction become disciplinary instead of advisory;

To finance the operation of the peace-keeping machinery and all the other activities deemed to be essential by the United Nations and its organs;

To take the political risks of possible failure and resultant danger to security;

To trust that the international control organization can and will defend against clandestinely prepared aggression.

It is obvious that many nations will at first find it almost unthinkable to move down the paths that will lead to such revolutionary changes in their traditions, beliefs, and senses of sovereignty. Yet how else can a warless world be achieved? Surely one cannot be so naïve as to suggest a system whereby each nation lays down its arms without any assurance that all other nations are doing likewise in strict conformity to the agreement. If we are to be confident in the permanence and security of our warless world then we will have to pay a heavy price for that confidence in terms of tradition, nationalism, and sovereignty.

Once we have paid the initial price, however, the loss will not weigh heavily on most of us, since supernationalism and hypersovereignty in some quarters have been one of the major threats to world peace. And so on the political front the world faces the great challenge: whether it wants warlessness enough to pay the price. Research in depth will be needed in all parts of the earth; unilateral and regional studies should be collated and summarized by United Nations experts, until there emerges a plan. Such a plan will not be a detailed blueprint, but should be sufficiently worked out so that each member of the world community can see, not only what is expected of itself and its friends, but what all the rest of the community is expected to do as well. A mutual recognition of the difficulties and possible sacrifices facing the whole family cannot fail to be of help.

*Economic possibilities*

One of the major arguments that still rages about the conclusion and operation of a world-disarmament agreement is that the economies, particularly of the Western nations, would undergo great transitional difficulties and would even fall into a sharp depression. (Several recent reports effectively challenge this view, notably "Economic Impacts of Disarmament," prepared for the United States Arms Control and Disarmament Agency by Professor Emil Benoit of Columbia University; and "Economic and Social Consequences of Disarmament," United Nations document number E/3593/Rev. I.) But regardless of fears, groundless or otherwise, there is and will be a rational concern for proper planning of the transition to the economy of a warless world. No one denies that to stop spending billions on armaments will affect the various economies, particularly of those nations whose disarmament task will be heavy. Equally one must concede that even among nations with a comparatively light disarmament job, the international repercussions generated by the transition of the great powers will make it necessary for the study and planning to be universal. Therefore, as pointed out by several of our authors, notably Kenneth Boulding and Grenville Clark, a great deal has to be learned before G & CD Day. And like so many subjects, that of economics involves different answers for different nations and areas and conditions of development. So, for each nation, in the light of its special situation, we will want to know, among other things:

How will warlessness affect the internal economy as a result of its own transition?

How will warlessness affect the internal economy as a result of the transition of others?

How will its changing economy affect the economy of the others?

What plans could and should be made now, in order to minimize all three effects?

What amelioration of transitional pains can we attribute to international organization such as the European Common Market? Should these be proliferated?

What should be the role of the United Nations Economic and Social Council? How does each nation tie into its regional ECOSOC?

Internally, what will happen to each major industry? What will happen to each industrial community?

How much of the savings due to disarmament can be applied to international-assistance programs? How much to debt reduction? Works projects? Education? Health and welfare? Tax reduction? Others?

What is the case load anticipated for retraining in the labor force?

We will not be able to get more than estimates as answers to some of these questions. In some of the developing countries the estimates themselves may be difficult if not impossible due to lack of statistical and other information. At the same time, the less developed countries have comparatively nonindustrial economies and should, therefore, be able to concentrate on raw-materials questions and less skilled-labor problems for their story. At all events, it will be an undertaking of great magnitude for each nation, plus a most formidable task for the international group which must pull the whole picture together. Yet if we are to escape economic dislocation of a serious kind, and if we are to apply the scores of billions saved by warlessness to their highest use, planning is the only answer. Planning, in turn, rests inexorably on knowledge of what is faced.

*Military possibilities*

Although the military posture is inextricable from the political in most cases, it should still be treated as a separate subject for our purposes. There is no doubt that few, if any, can visualize their own country without a military arm, with the exception of the nationals of those few nations whose armed forces are considered adequate only for internal security. We of the United States have not been a particularly militaristic people, but, at least since World War I, the idea of strong armed forces has become generally accepted and in many cases revered by those who believe deterrence to be synonymous with world peace.

However, on G & CD Day, the only deterrence in sight will be the International Peace Force, since by agreement national forces will have shrunk to internal police proportions. One could speculate at great length on the preparations that must take place before we actually put a disarmament plan into effect. These will have been thrashed out in each nation before the agreement is reached, and we can assume that, once the decision has been made that the price is worth the gain, there will be comparatively little difficulty with the details of progressively destroying the national military machines. To some it will be like pulling teeth; to others a great relief; to most, perhaps, a matter of uneasiness and wonder.

In the United States, we will without doubt have to say good-by to the military, naval, and air-force academies which now loom large on the scene. One academy, greatly reduced in numbers of students, will probably suffice. The Pentagon nearly empty; most of the posts, camps, and stations abandoned; parades and fly-overs discontinued; bases both domestic and far-flung deactivated—many and varied activities to which we have become accustomed will disappear. It will be a strange world, hard to get used to, difficult and sometimes painful to plan for. And the questions to be answered are most difficult, revolving around the proper size of our military establishment and the number and type of weapons that will be needed.

But new challenges to our ingenuity emerge even as we plan for the destruction of our national deterrence, for we must study with the greatest care the creation, constitution, and operation of the international body which will take its place. Here literally scores of difficult matters will have to be resolved, and resolved in such a way that all the nations concerned can acquiesce in the decision. To mention only a few of the questions that must be answered:

How large a force will be required, in terms of men, munitions, ships, tanks, planes?

Should every country furnish either personnel or supplies, and who will decide how much?

Should personnel act on a solely international basis or do

they retain national entity? By whom and on what scale should they be paid?

Should the force be kept at United Nations stations or remain available at home bases?

Should specific forces be assigned or should pools be made available by the contributing nations?

Should the top command and staff be made up of the best available talent or should they consist of "nonaligned" nationals only?

Who will decide what elements of the force will be used in any specific country or area? Who will decide on the nationality of command officers in the field?

Where should weapons and material for the force be procured? What types of weapons will be necessary and who will decide that?

Should the permanent members of the Security Council be exempted from furnishing personnel or weapons?

What ground rules should be established for use of the force? Will it act only in cases of threatened aggression, or at threats of armed rebellion?

It will not be easy to find the answers, given the best will in the world, to these and many other details of policy and organization and operation. That is why so much study is needed in advance. Perhaps our military people could sit down and estimate the maximum forces needed for internal security in each of the nations of the world, but I rather doubt that every nation would agree with the strength assigned to it by such a system. An arrangement may be necessary whereby all nations make their own estimates and allow a representative international group to work out a balance on the basis of the lowest common denominator. At any rate, the key word for all these troubles is preparation, and still more preparation.

### Educational and informational possibilities

In the change of orientation called for in this volume, the field of education and public information must play a vital part. This applies not only to the research studies that must be made, but to the whole complex of the educational systems of the world, in helping condition people of all ages to the new concepts that must be embraced in order to make possible the warlessness which is sought.

Jules Moch speaks of the intrinsic human appetite for war; the social basis of conflict. Judd Marmor discusses a whole range of revisions needed in our education of the young. Walter Millis speaks of the revolution of expectations. Grenville Clark suggests a study of possible distribution of available funds between the Peace Force, the standard of living, and the standard of education. Arthur Larson speaks of promotion of change by law and the need for change in education as well as other factors in the problems that remain to be solved. And so it goes, with general appreciation on the part of all the authors that education per se must receive weighty attention in any plans that are to be made.

The questions that are posed by this major factor are not as clear and obvious as those concerning the Peace Force, but a few will suffice to give an impression of the needs of our warless world planners:

How teach public opinion that a warless world is possible, sensible, and safe?

How revise the study of history in order to de-emphasize the wars and the battles and re-emphasize the changes and trends in human institutions?

What place in a warless world will a common language take? What should the language be and who should decide?

What organization should be responsible for the foundation of a system of truly international universities?

Who should be in charge of vastly expanded student exchange programs?

How shall we organize a vast program of adult education on matters of international cooperation?

How are we to make sure that educational systems are not subverted to cause a turn toward extreme nationalism?

How can education and information best treat the "creeping sickness of hate"?

How can education and entertainment reverse the desensiti-
zation to violence now produced in movies, television,
and other media?

It is apparent that the responsibility of education and information must be heaviest, at the outset, at those age levels
where certain beliefs, or perhaps we should say prejudices, will
have to be *unlearned* before people will accept the idea of a
warless world. This does not mean that no attention need be paid
to the kindergarten—it is obviously sensible that the younger
children not acquire such prejudices in the first place. But as we
move to prepare ourselves for G & CD Day, one of our major
difficulties will be to persuade people that such a thing is to their
own selfish advantage. Individuals who stoutly proclaim their
desire for peace are often inclined to belligerence at a wrong,
whether real or fancied. Many have never lost the juvenile conviction that the only way to win an argument is to beat your
opponent physically. One can hope that M. Moch is right when
he states that in the twentieth century the "taste for war" is dead.
I have too recent a memory of many Americans, some of them
prominent, advocating that the United States go into Cuba and
subdue the Castro regime and the Cuban people with overwhelming military force.

Education and information, then, have perhaps the gravest
responsibility of all: that of creating an attitude which can in
turn create an atmosphere in which a warless world can be
achieved. And this will be no easy task. Belligerence has been
creating counterbelligerence for many years, and the "creeping
sickness of hate" is so widespread an epidemic that virtually no
corner of the earth is immune to it.

*Sociological possibilities*

Many factors in the sociological field impinge on the other
areas already discussed, but there are nevertheless certain problems to be solved before G & CD Day which do not fit into any
other pattern. Matters of population control, dislocation of labor
forces, social systems as possible models of warlessness, and the

like thrust themselves out for attention in the preceding chapters. Here is a partial listing of the most obvious questions:

What, in general, should take the place of war in order to satisfy the "conflict urge" in society? Will contact sports be enough?

How important to warlessness is the control of population explosion? Will rising standards of living help?

How make planned parenthood totally acceptable in all parts of the world?

What scope of relocation of labor is necessary or possible in the event of shutdown of defense plants?

Apart from labor, what are the sociological implications of economic reaction to warlessness?

What is the impact upon modern society of continuous crisis and pressure? Does youth react positively to the threat of possible fatal military service?

Does society as a whole have recognizable reactions to war versus peace, democracy versus dictatorship, etc., and can these be called upon to provide platforms for study and action?

It can easily be seen that a great many additional questions can be posed in this field, having to do with the struggle of ideas and values and the moral, psychological, and spiritual problems which are bound to arise. Anything that affects human life so strongly that there will be little fear of its ending through war, is bound to bring about more questions than answers. Whatever may be the moral equivalent of war, it must certainly affect people even more than institutions. If younger people are headed now into hopelessness for the future, what will happen during the moral and psychological regeneration that will certainly accompany the ultimate recognition that hopelessness has suddenly disappeared?

One more thought, about people. We have become conditioned, of late, to the idea that the human spirit is capable of withstanding such fantastic pessimistic pressures as to defy the usual norms of value. What, then, is to happen if these pressures are relaxed in a short space of time? Will there be a possibility that moral fiber will toughen, or will we become prey to the blandishment that may take the place of missile rattling? Today the obvious answer is nonexistent. If we were to realize suddenly that we could no longer rely on armaments, would we become weaker or stronger? One obviously plumps for the latter, since adaptability to new conditions should never spell weakness when confronted with the new threat. At the same time, we just do not know. We should and must put brain power to work on it, because it is so apparent that emotion is not enough.

## *Legal possibilities*

In taking up this final division, I find comfort in the fact since it is generally agreed that real change can take place only within a framework of law, one must study the law to find out where it needs strengthening in order to encompass the change. Granted, as Arthur Larson points out, that much has been put behind us already, and that the rule that agreements must be kept has already caused vast changes, there are still elements of doubt about some of the legal implications of a warless world.

Of particular importance is the encircling arm to protect the whole complex of peace-keeping machinery. Although certain legal questions were implied in the discussion under "military possibilities," we may consider these further points:

Will any changes be needed in the United Nations Charter or in any of its rules and regulations in order to give required authority to the Peace Force?

Will there be need for any changes in the constitutions, laws, or treaties of any nation in order to furnish personnel or material to the Peace Force?

Will there be need for changes in the constitutions, laws, or treaties of any nation in order to allow the Peace Force to operate within or from within its borders?

What standardization is possible of national laws or international agreements affecting manufacture, transportation, and delivery of illicit armaments? What strengthening is needed?

Need national laws on illicit military supplies be adjusted to allow for international enforcement?

Would any changes be necessary in citizenship laws and regulations as a result of recruitment for a purely international force to serve in various parts of the world?

Many additional questions may occur which have no relation to the International Peace Force but which impinge on the legal side. Among these might be:

What changes, international and national, will be required to make the decisions of the International Court of Justice binding rather than advisory? Should these changes be made?

What legal steps will be necessary to embark on a wide campaign of population control? Would legal action be preferable or complementary to education?

How can the substantive rules and principles of international law be more effectively universalized, and thus made more acceptable to all parts of the world?

All the foregoing is not intended to be, nor can it be, an exhaustive examination of the problems of preparing to move from today's tensions to a world without war. We should leave such an examination to the experts in each field who can and should develop research and study designs to be followed by the national and international groups charged with the action programs. It should suffice, however, to give us some intimation of the scope of the preparatory work that must be completed. Only if the work is begun now can we hope to escape the shame of the fabled yokel, who, after repeatedly trying without success to direct a lost motorist to his destination, finally blurted: "Mister, yuh just can't get there from here!"

# The Russian idea of a world without arms

Explanation: On June 12, 1962, a month after the symposium on "A Warless World" was announced in the *Saturday Review* and initiated with the article by Arnold Toynbee, a discussion on a future world without arms was held in Moscow at the editorial offices of *International Affairs,* the monthly journal of the Soviet Society for the Popularisation of Political and Scientific Knowledge.

The discussion was published in English in the July, 1962, issue of *International Affairs.* With a few small cuts (none of substance) it is reproduced here, in the thought that a comparison of this discussion and that of *A Warless World* will prove interesting, both as to the substantive ideas expressed, and as to the approach, tone, and emphasis of the various statements.

Those taking part in the discussion were: Sh. Sanakoyev, Cand. Sc. (Hist.); F. Kozhevnikov, D.Sc. (Law); Corresponding Member of the Academy of Sciences of the U.S.S.R., Y. Korovin; L. Gromov, researcher at the Institute of World Economy and International Relations; V. Strigachev, Cand. Sc. (Econ.); V. Rymalov, Cand. Sc. (Econ.); Maj.-Gen. M. Goryainov, Cand. Sc. (Tech.); Maj.-Gen. S. Pokrovsky, D.Sc. (Tech.); and Maj.-Gen. N. Talensky, D.Sc. (Mil.).

## Our idea of a world without arms

SH. SANAKOYEV: Today we have decided to cast a glance at the world of tomorrow, a world without arms. I suggest ... that we share our ideas about this world, and the development of international relations after plans for general and complete disarmament are adopted and implemented. In other words, let us give thought today to the prospects, the direction and paths along which international developments may or can go.

We are, of course, aware of the immense difficulties involved in reaching a disarmament solution and of the stubborn resistance certain circles in the imperialist countries, particularly in America, will put up. We also realise that our partners in the talks do not find it so easy to imagine the future of the old world—the capitalist system —without the continual maintenance of its armed strength directed against its own peoples and without the profits which the capitalist monopolies get from the arms drive.

However, objective conditions now exist in the world which increasingly require a *rational* approach to the disarmament problem. The main condition is the new relation of forces in the world which is far from being to the advantage of the capitalist system. Thanks to this—and this is due in no small measure to the military superiority of the Soviet Union and the other peace-loving states—a new situation has arisen in the world in which imperialism is no longer able to resort to a general war, as in the past, without risking its existence.

Besides, the policy of the arms race and preparation for war, which is of the very nature of imperialism, has in present-day conditions driven the imperialist camp into a blind alley. Although it has created a vast war machine, imperialism today has very limited possibilities for setting it in motion. Thus their fear of nuclear-missile warfare and their anxiety for the future of their system compels the present leaders of the imperialist Powers to hold talks about disarmament.

Speeches by Western leaders contain numerous hypocritical statements about their "desire for peace" and even incantations against war. On the question of preserving peace, as on the question of disarmament, we should, in Lenin's words, like to "see as little as possible of general statements, solemn promises, or splendid formulas, and as much as possible of the simplest and clearest decisions and measures actually leading to peace. . . ."

Regardless of the evasions to which the rulers of the Western Powers resort, the objective development of human society has confronted them with this inescapable alternative: either a nuclear-missile war inevitably ending in the final destruction of the capitalist system, or recognition of the peaceful co-existence of states with different socio-economic systems. Peaceful co-existence leads to an improvement of the international situation, an end to the arms drive and the cold war policy. It is the stepping stone that can help mankind to stride over the *barrier,* leaving behind it a world in arms and entering a world without arms.

What will this unknown world without arms be like? What must it be like?

After disarmament, the development of world affairs would naturally enter a new phase. There would be serious, I should say, quantitative changes in the world, the international situation would be normalised, many factors of tension would disappear, and confidence between states would be strengthened.

A characteristic feature of a world without arms will unquestionably be wider and fuller practice of the principles of peaceful coexistence in relations between Socialist and capitalist countries. Implementation of plans for general and complete disarmament will rid international affairs of such phenomena as the arms drive and mistrust between states; the "positions of strength" and the cold war policy, which aggressive circles in the West are now using as a weapon in preparing for war and organising all kinds of reckless military gambles, will lose all meaning.

The need—and what is most important, the possibility—of resorting to force of arms in settling issues will disappear. Negotiations will become the *only* method of settling any disputes between states.

A disarmed world will create suitable conditions for the observance of such an important principle as non-interference in the internal affairs of states and respect for the sovereignty and national independence of all countries and peoples, big and small. It is no secret that at present talk about the sovereignty and equal rights of states in the capitalist part of the world is, putting it mildly, purely ritualistic.

Can there be any equality between U.S. imperialism, which is armed to the teeth, and the Latin American countries, underdeveloped economically and militarily, most of which are under the complete economic domination of the U.S. monopolies? Can one talk of the full sovereignty of most of the West European NATO countries whose foreign policy is not shaped in their capitals? Is it surprising that such a foreign policy is in direct contradiction to their national interest? The present-day capitalist world is dominated by a cult of strength; the imperialist Powers and their monopolies dictate their will—in the fullest sense of the word.

In the world of tomorrow, in which there will no longer be any armed forces or military superiority of one country over others, the objective conditions for violations of sovereignty and national independence will disappear, and rapid economic and cultural development of once backward peoples will become possible; this will unquestionably further accelerate the development of the whole of human society. Incidentally, it is my belief that one of the main reasons for the sabotage by the top leaders of the United States of any solution of the disarmament problem is their desire to retain, at any cost, their *diktat* over other countries and domination of the capitalist world by their monopolies.

After disarmament new, favourable conditions will arise in the world for a truly peaceful competition between the two systems, Socialism and capitalism. We are sure that this will give our system the opportunity of demonstrating much more forcibly its superiority over capitalism and of showing all men that the future of mankind lies in Communism, which proclaims Peace, Labour, Freedom, Equality, Fraternity and Happiness for all peoples on earth.

F. KOZHEVNIKOV: Our chairman Sanakoyev was quite right in saying that in a world without arms there will be universal acceptance of the peaceful principles of international relations. Accordingly, international bodies, the United Nations above all, will become genuine instruments of universal peace; the various methods of peaceful settlement of any contradictions between states will acquire a new social purpose.

It is a well-known fact that the Soviet Union is prepared to accept any system of controls and guarantees in a world that is disarming, provided the Western Powers sign a treaty on general and complete disarmament. The Draft Treaty of March 15, 1962, envisages a clear-cut and effective system of controls and guarantees on the fulfilling of disarmament obligations. This system rests on the joint statement of agreed principles of disarmament accepted by the U.S.S.R. and the United States between June and September 1961. These principles provide, in particular, for measures "to strengthen institutions for the maintenance of peace and the settlement of international disputes by peaceful means."

In connection with the problem of general and complete disarmament Western statesmen and public leaders, politicians and jurists have put forward various projects for reorganising the present legal order. Endorsing the idea of general and complete disarmament, at least in words, some of them propose that the world legal order should be reorganised as a preliminary to disarmament; others insist that this be done simultaneously with disarmament; still others believe that such a reorganisation should be done after disarmament, i.e., in a disarmed world.

Thus, the leaders of the World Parliament Association, who came to Moscow last year, and with whom we had a useful exchange of opinion, expressed the following ideas about disarmament. They believe that to attain this ideal the United Nations must be drastically remodelled in order to set up:

1. a World Parliament to enact world laws in order to secure and maintain permanent peace;

2. an Executive to administer these laws;

3. International Courts of Justice with compulsory jurisdiction in all matters of dispute concerning these world laws;

4. a world police force to enforce world laws against all those who commit, or threaten to commit, a breach of these world laws;

and by these means to secure universal simultaneous and complete disarmament of all nations.

The prominent American jurists and public figures Clark and Sohn, in their interesting book *World Peace Through World Law,* incline to the idea of a simultaneous process of disarmament and the setting up of an effective world police force. In their opinion, other appropriate world organs should be set up on that basis, including an effective judicial or judicial-type system, a world economic development administration, the necessary world legislative and executive organs, and also a system of providing revenue for these purposes.

I think, first of all, that no preliminary conditions should be set for disarmament; the proposed reorganisation of the world legal order is unrealistic, and is unacceptable in principle, for it clashes with contemporary international law which is based on the principles of the peaceful co-existence of states with different social systems and the sovereignty and sovereign equality of all countries. In substance, these plans for a world law, a world parliament, and world executive and judicial organs mean the abolition of international law, based on the principles of the co-ordination, and not of the subordination, of the sovereign wills of states and peoples.

Y. KOROVIN: It is a very remarkable and curious fact that many Western political leaders and even scientists and scholars, conditioned to the cold war atmosphere for years, find it hard to imagine a disarmed world, and forecast innumerable and inevitable difficulties in the way of its emergence.

Some, such as H. Brown, say these difficulties spring from human nature and man's "inability" to rebuild political and social relations to conform to a world without arms, and wars. Others, like Prof. Th. Schelling of Harvard University, give themselves up to sceptical ruminations, asserting that the despotic states of antiquity were much better able than modern states to combat mutual mistrust and international tension (exchange of hostages and spies, intermarriage of dynasties, etc.). In an article in *Foreign Affairs,* with the eloquent title, "The Role of Deterrence in Total Disarmament", he questions the practical possibility of disarmament inasmuch as after the destruction of military planes, rockets and other delivery vehicles, even "a donkey becomes a means of delivery". Moreover, he says, a lover of military gambles may at any moment become the head of some country, while the international armed forces, designed to serve as a guarantee of universal security, may themselves become the source of a new threat of war.

In the final analysis, Schelling and people like him, turn general disarmament into a utopia, and into a very "harmful" one at that, because, as Edward Teller, "the father of the American hydrogen bomb", assures us, international control connected with disarmament "will give rise to suspicions and to friction", and will "become a source of irritation", in consequence of which "disarmament may lead to frustration, friction and failure" . . . .

Having scared themselves and others by such sinister prospects, American and British scientists and politicians have started an intensive search for original kinds of guarantees against the "dangers" of disarmament. Thus Prof. A. Larson, in his work, *Arms Control Through World Law,* says that it is urgently necessary to draw up an international code of law obligatory for all. It should, in addition, be supplemented by a "code of co-existence" which "would define in precise form those activities of states which would no longer be permitted".

A number of public and scientific organisations in the West have put in considerable efforts to elaborate the organisational forms and activity of international organs of coercion in a disarmed world. In this connection special attention is given to the problem of organising international armed forces, which are regarded as the chief guarantee against eventual aggression by any disarmed state. The point of departure in this reasoning is the hypothesis that such a state would preserve its capacity for aggressive acts, making use of concealed or secretly accumulated weapons and/or a preponderance in its police forces or population, even if armed with the most primitive weapons.

The many Western projects provide for various methods of formation of international armed forces (either from units of all states, or from the Great Powers, or from the small states); different numerical strength (from several tens of thousands to a million and more men); various points of their deployment (in the most threatened areas of the world, at special U.N. military bases, or scattered all over the world); various versions of their armament (from small arms to nuclear weapons); and various forms of their leadership and command.

I think that the basic flaw in all these conceptions is that their authors fail to understand the real causes of aggressions and wars, and in consequence, underestimate the effects of general and complete disarmament.

Let us take a look, for example, as to how the authors of the book *World Peace Through World Law* explain what is blocking general and complete disarmament. They think that the first and most important obstacle is the "reluctance of the average person to make any drastic change in his traditional form of behaviour", or in other words, habit and routine. They add: "The units into which mankind has combined—family, tribe, town, city, national state—have been accustomed to assert or defend their interests, real or supposed, by violence or the threat of it."

The second obstacle, the authors say, is the military profession, "which in many nations has sufficient influence to force their Governments to resist rather than to aid the cause of total disarmament". The authors do not explain that this is because the military leaders are connected with the war corporations and have a vested financial interest in them. They say instead that it is due to their professional "training" and the idea that their profession is "indispensable". That is the third reason.

Fourth comes the "adverse influence" of traditional diplomacy brought up on the habits of Great Power politics. In fifth place is another category of " 'vested interest' ... an important obstacle to disarmament and peace is the presumed interest of many millions of armament workers in a continuance of their jobs"; this is placed on the same level with the "interest of proprietors in their profits from armament contracts".

Finally, the most serious obstacle of all: "mutual fears and recriminations", dividing the East and the West, and the "poisoned atmosphere" in which their relations develop.

I have given their reasoning in sufficient detail because each of its links is either false in substance or, at best, takes the cause for the effect.

Is there any need to prove that it is not in the nature of the "average person" to destroy his fellow beings but that, on the contrary, he yearns for a life of peace and tranquillity for himself and his near ones? The negative role of the military and diplomats in some capitalist countries is beyond question, but it is negative because they are the agents of monopoly capital, which carries on the frenzied arms drive in its race for superprofits.

As for the "interest" of armament workers in the prosperity of the war industry, the authors are forced to admit that in the process of general disarmament, apart from a possible reduction of taxes and the development of peaceful construction aimed at higher living standards for broad sections of the population, the war industry can be remodelled to turn out peacetime products, with an appropriate relocation of labour and means of production.

The cold war atmosphere in all its manifestations undoubtedly serves as an obstacle to disarmament. But the cold war itself is no meteor fallen from the skies due to causes beyond human control; it is the outcome of a definite political course imposed by persons and groups which are interested in it being carried through.

In trying to outline the real contours of international relations in a world without arms, we should proceed above all from the fact that disarmament itself would create an entirely new international climate, an atmosphere of confidence and co-operation. This does not, of course, mean that the conflicts and frictions dividing the states will disappear as if by magic. They will remain so long as there exists an antagonistic society with all its contradictions and struggles, both internal and international. But with general disarmament the forms of these struggles will undergo substantial change.

Putting it into the language of international law, a disarmed world will be not only rid of all the methods of settling international conflicts by force, but the means of peaceful settlement of international disputes will acquire a new quality. Diplomatic negotiations and consultations at all levels (right up to the top), commissions of inquiry and conciliation, and mediation, arbitration and the international court will be quite different. The disappearance of the possibility of settling differences between states by force will inevitably enhance the importance of all kinds of peaceful legal procedures; instead of being optional many of them will become compulsory, and instead of casual, habitual.

In short, all this will considerably enhance the role of international law in international relations, and will turn it into a permanent code of peaceful co-existence, embracing the numerous aspects of relations between states with different social systems. The states will be faced with the following alternative: either no solution of the disputes arising between them, or settlement by peaceful diplomatic and legal methods.

In a disarmed world, the nature of diplomacy itself will change. Since the diplomacy of military blocs, threats and blackmail will disappear together with the weapons, the diplomatic service will become a means of strengthening and developing international co-operation, a kind of co-ordinating centre uniting and directing the steadily expanding forms of this co-operation—in politics, the economy, science, culture, etc.

F. KOZHEVNIKOV: I am convinced that the fundamentals of contemporary international law should not only be preserved but strengthened in a disarmed world. This applies, I think, also to the basic principles of international justice, which must, however, be improved.

Thus, the International Court of Justice of the United Nations must truly ensure the representation of the chief forms of civilisation and major legal systems of the world.

This important provision remains on paper. There is no doubt at all that the law of the Chinese People's Republic ranks among the major legal systems of the world, but on the bench of the Court there is no citizen of the Chinese People's Republic. Obviously, the restoration of the legitimate rights of the Chinese People's Republic in all U.N. organs must, as a matter of course, entail representation of China's civilisation and her legal system in the International Court. Only a judge who is a citizen of the Chinese People's Republic can be a member of the International Court of Justice from China.

At present, almost all the Socialist countries are parties to its Statute. In view of this, the systems of Socialist law must have fuller representation in the International Court. As with all U.N. organs, there must be fairer representation of the Socialist system and the neutral countries in the International Court of the world. The jurisdiction of the Court comprises all legal disputes between states on the basis of free and reciprocal recognition of its legal jurisdiction. This principle must be retained. Of course, states may declare that they recognise the compulsory jurisdiction of the Court unconditionally or with reservations. The right to make reservations is an incontestable sovereign right, but no reservation should clash with the Statute of the Court. However, this does happen in practice. Thus in recognising the jurisdiction of the Court as compulsory, some say that it does not extend to disputes which in substance fall within the sphere of "national competence", as construed or defined by the state in question.

The first such formula was put forward by the United States (August 26, 1946), and later by the Union of South Africa and several other countries. It should be noted that the said reservation drew strong objections from many jurists, including American.

Or take the Portuguese reservation. In its statement (on December 19, 1955) recognising the compulsory jurisdiction of the International Court of Justice, the Portuguese Government reserved the right to exclude from the sphere of application of the said declaration, at any time it remained in force, one or many definite categories of disputes. Doubt as to the conformity of the Portuguese reservation to Article 36, Paragraph 2 of the Statute was expressed, for instance, by the Swedish Government. Its statement to the U.N. Secretary-General (February 23, 1956) was to the effect that the said Portuguese reservation was incompatible with recognition of the jurisdiction of the Court as compulsory. A similar stand in this respect was taken by the Government of India in connection with the question of the right of transit across India's territory.

The Court itself should be more consistent in applying the generally accepted principles of contemporary international law. Unfortunately, that is not always the case.

Y. KOROVIN: I am not inclined to attach too much importance to the need for setting up international armed forces in a disarmed world. Increased pressure from the broad masses of the people on the foreign policies of states, together with strict day-to-day control over disarmament—as general and complete as disarmament itself —will serve as a sufficiently sound guarantee against open or secret remilitarisation, the inevitable precursor and concomitant of aggression.

This matter has been discussed in detail in our press, in particular, in *International Affairs* (Nos. 4 and 5 for 1960) and at international scientific meetings (for example, the Pugwash Conferences of Scientists, and the East-West Round Table). I shall, therefore, confine myself to just a few ideas.

Let us assume, as a hypothesis, that a disarmed state, making use of its great population, or its preponderance in police forces, is either threatening a weaker state or is violating its frontiers. The question is whether or not there is need of a World Government and the maintenance of a permanent international army to settle such an incident?

I think that the U.N. Charter now in force, and the Soviet Union's Draft Treaty on General and Complete Disarmament (1962) hold out much simpler and quite effective formulas for averting such developments which in a disarmed world would be pathological. I have in mind Chapter VII of the U.N. Charter (Action with Respect to Threats to Peace, Breaches of the Peace and Acts of Aggression) and Articles 18, 27, 36, 37 and 38 of the Soviet Draft Treaty on Disarmament.

It is proposed that at the first and second stages of general and complete disarmament the state parties to the Treaty should conclude special agreements with the U.N. Security Council (in conformity with Article 43 of the U.N. Charter) on making available to the Security Council, at its request, definite units of national armed forces.

These forces, exceeding in the aggregate the armed forces of any would-be aggressor, would apparently be quite sufficient to crush the resistance of an aggressor, apart from the fact that the latter would be subjected to the whole system of U.N. sanctions, ranging from the severance of diplomatic relations to complete economic boycott.

At the third stage of disarmament, i.e., after the national armed forces have been disbanded, the states would have at their disposal strictly limited units of police (militia) equipped with small arms. The International Organisation would also control the areas of their deployment, any considerable movements on their part, their numerical strength, their armaments and arms manufacture. When necessary, the states would have to make available to the Security Council, at its request, appropriate units of the national police (militia) forces. The size of these formations and the area of their deployment would be determined under agreements between the Security Council and the states concerned.

Any possibility of the unilateral use of international armed forces in the interests of one state or group of states would be ruled out by the structure of their command formed from representatives of the three main groups of states existing in the world today, and operating by way of mutual agreement.

I think that the implementation of general and complete disarmament under strict international control, combined with the measures outlined above, would be the most reliable and quite a realistic guarantee of stable and inviolable peace on earth, humanity's age-long dream. That is why there is no need to overload the ship of a disarmed world with such additional freight as a world government with its collective militarism and world bureaucracy of all ranks and types.

SH. SANAKOYEV: We have listened with interest to the opinions of our colleagues, the jurists, but that is naturally only one aspect of the problem under discussion. Now it's the turn of our economists.

L. GROMOV: I wish to speak on the subject that interests me most of all—the problem of employment and work in a disarmed world.

War preparations—whether undertaken for frankly aggressive aims, as in the member states of Western military and political blocs, or dictated by the need to defend the great gains of the peoples in countries which are either building Socialism and Communism or have recently emerged from colonial oppression—everywhere divert large numbers of people, their knowledge and energies to the production and application of means of destruction and annihilation. This is a colossal waste of the most precious capital mankind has, which is, moreover, fraught with the danger of mass annihilation.

Almost 100 million men are now engaged in servicing and improving the modern war machine and keeping it ready for action. This is a powerful, potentially creative force, comprising that part of mankind which is endowed with greater than average youthful vigour, energy and knowledge. It includes tens of millions of uniformed young men in their prime and tens of millions of skilled and experienced workers and hundreds of thousands, if not millions, of engineers and scientists.

Indeed, if men who are the cream of the present generation could apply all the instruments of labour they now use for war in peaceful pursuits, this peaceful army, 100-million strong, could perform miracles in the shortest imaginable space of time; it could transform continents, subdue the ocean and outer space, conquer diseases, gain control of the micro-world and make it serve man. Nor is this a utopia. This gives a general picture of the benefits general and complete disarmament could bring mankind if the peoples bring sufficient pressure to bear on those rulers who are heading for war to make them stop the machine busy preparing for war and regear it to peace.

But is mankind capable of making use of these opportunities? After all, in the countries where capitalism with its greed and quest for profits is often an insuperable obstacle to the correct employment of the labour force, millions of people there cannot find work for years on end. Surely the fact that in these countries tens of millions of people are engaged in war preparations and are thus able to earn their daily bread should be regarded as a blessing? Might not disarmament take their jobs from them and even worsen the lot of those who today are pursuing peaceful occupations?

There are many people in the West who endlessly reiterate these arguments "No butter without rockets"—they keep on repeating so as to din into the mind of the ordinary workingman the idea that the arms race does not mean war—yet—but bread, while disarmament will inevitably bring unemployment and starvation. How depraved are those people who, in order to keep their profits, want to link work and death in an unbreakable chain! These gentlemen are not really worried about the people's bread and butter, but about the fat dividends war orders bring them.

Yet, science and history both prove that even in states where the capitalist system prevents the full employment of labour resources, it is possible to carry out measures which will not only help draw into socially useful labour all who will be released by disarmament from working for war, but will also increase general employment and thereby improve the lot of the working people in general.

After the Second World War when the reduction of the armed forces and the regearing of the economy to peacetime needs proceeded on a much larger scale and at a faster rate than envisaged in our programme for general and complete disarmament, unemployment throughout the West dropped far below the pre-war level and general employment greatly exceeded that level. The existence of specific favourable conditions in that period does not minimise the importance of the special governmental measures undertaken to ease the return to peaceful occupations of people who serviced the war machine.

Similar measures, although better thought out, more detailed and constituting an integral part of national disarmament plans, are fully able in present-day conditions to ensure the switching-over of labour from the war machine to peaceful endeavours, which will not only be a painless but also a beneficial process for the working people in the West.

This proposition is confirmed in calculations by some very competent economists (in the United States, for example, Leontief, Perlo, Lumer and others) and in the assessment made by a Consultative Group under the U.N. Secretary-General, which early this year submitted a report on the *Economic and Social Consequences of Disarmament*. This report makes a detailed examination of the general and social problems of employment in the Western countries in relation to disarmament. It points to the full possibility of solving these problems painlessly and recommends measures necessary for realising these possibilities which are within the reach of all Governments. Eminent economists who drew up the report make the following indisputable conclusion:

"The Consultative Group is unanimously of the opinion that all the problems and difficulties of transition connected with disarmament could be met by appropriate national and international measures. There should thus be no doubt that the diversion to peaceful purposes of the resources now in military use could be accomplished to the benefit of all countries and lead to the improvement of world economic and social conditions. The achievement of general and complete disarmament would be an unqualified blessing to all mankind".

It is clear that in the Socialist countries where full employment was achieved long ago, where there is no unemployment and where all resources are used in a planned way in the interest of the people, the switch-over of servicemen and citizens now working for defence to peaceful labour as a result of general and complete disarmament will proceed much faster and more efficiently than in the Western countries.

This is generally recognised and is stressed in the U.N. report on problems of disarmament. It points out, for example, that "no significant problems were created" by the substantial reduction of armed forces in the Socialist countries (called in the report "the centrally planned economies") in 1955–1958 and stresses that "the replies of Governments of the centrally planned economies [to questions about the economic aspects of disarmament.—L.G.] state that there will be no difficulties in absorbing the released [as a result of disarmament.—L.G.] manpower".

Thus, general and complete disarmament will not only bring the peoples the greatest blessing of our time—peace, but will also enrich the peaceful labour of mankind with additional exceptionally valuable resources and will give a fresh stimulus to the economic and cultural progress of society.

V. Strigachev: The question just discusssed by my colleague is closely bound up with another one—capital investments in a disarmed world.

The money now spent for military purposes by all states is equal to approximately half of that part of their gross national income which now goes on capital investments. Since war preparations include large-scale construction work—industrial, road, housing, etc. —it is clear that the arms race greatly curtails the possibilities of capital investments of a peaceful character.

In comparison with capital investments, military expenditure is particularly large in the principal Western countries, which are members of military alignments. Thus, on the evidence of U.N. experts, average direct military expenditure in 1957–1959 in comparison with investments in fixed assets amounted to 58.3 per cent in the United States, 34.7 per cent in France, 42.1 per cent in Great Britain, 18.4 per cent in Canada and 16.7 per cent in the Federal Republic of Germany.

The ratio is also quite high in underdeveloped countries which have been drawn into imperialist military blocs: 18.3 per cent in Turkey, 29.5 per cent in Greece, 19.5 per cent in Portugal, 21.5 per cent in Thailand, 19.7 per cent in the Philippines and 57.8 per cent in South Korea.

Countries which have fairly recently gained their national independence or are now completing the liberation of their territory, or are protecting their security from colonialist intrigues, are also compelled to make large military outlays relative to investments in the economy.

Thus, general and complete disarmament will give vast opportunities to expand investments in production, in various economic and cultural services and in the development of science and technology.

The need for such investments is quite great, as can be seen in the case of the developed capitalist countries, for example, the richest Western country, the United States of America.

According to estimates of the National Planning Association, published in March 1960, in order to satisfy the most urgent needs of the American people $330,000 million would need to be spent in five years, including $30,000 million on education, $75,000 million on the transport services, $100,000 million on urban improvement and housing, $60,000 million on water supplies and the conservation of water resources, $35,000 million on the public health services and $30,000 million on other measures (purification of air, development of research, etc.).

Annual expenditure for these purposes, mainly in the sphere of capital investment, would come to about $66,000 million, as against their actual level of $30,000 million. Clearly, a large part of the missing $36,000 million could be covered by the budget following on disarmament. One consequence of such large-scale public construction would be the demand for additional private investments in the building industry, various branches of the engineering industry, etc.

The need of the underdeveloped countries in capital investments is still greater. Disarmament will open up especially favourable prospects for them.

Now I will go on to discuss the prospects disarmament holds out for the Socialist countries which do not suffer from underemployment of production capacity and need large capital construction to carry out their sweeping plans.

These countries have to protect their great achievements and their military expenditure is large both in absolute terms and in comparison with capital investments. The Economic and Social Consequences of Disarmament report states that military expenditure in the Soviet Union is equivalent to 34.4 per cent of capital investments, in the Chinese People's Republic to 27.8 per cent, in Czechoslovakia to 28 per cent, etc. General and complete disarmament will naturally release huge funds in these countries for additional capital outlays. The planned economies of the Socialist states will ensure the swift and efficient employment of these additional resources in their national economy and for accomplishing the previously mentioned international tasks.

General and complete disarmament, consequently, will create the conditions for a great and fairly swift expansion of that part of mankind's wealth which is embodied in its capital assets and thereby raise the material and cultural standards of the people.

V. RYMALOV: What Strigachev said applies also to the underdeveloped countries of Asia, Africa, Latin America and Oceania which until quite recently were completely excluded from deciding the main international questions. The peoples of these countries are becoming another powerful force for peace.

One of the most urgent tasks facing the underdeveloped countries is to *destroy colonialism finally and completely in all its forms and manifestations, and a disarmed world will provide the most favourable conditions for doing this.* To begin with, in a disarmed world imperialism will finally be deprived of the possibility of waging aggressive colonial wars against peoples fighting for their independence. Peaceful co-existence, which is destined to become the basic principle of international relations, presupposes non-interference in the domestic affairs of other countries, the granting to all peoples without exception of the right to self-determination and the right to decide their own future.

Thus disarmament, far from retarding, actually accelerates the great revolutionary changes under way in underdeveloped countries. The protracted agony of colonialism, which is still fraught with immeasurable calamities and suffering for mankind, will be less painful and will not exact fresh huge sacrifices from the peoples.

The peoples of the underdeveloped countries know that a society without arms and war will inevitably become a society without colonial and national oppression. There will be no room in it for such disgraceful concepts as "colonies" or "non-self-governing territories". Scores of millions of people still kept by force of arms in colonial bondage will be able to achieve independence without delay and without needless sacrifices. These are not the only political results however which general and complete disarmament will produce by stimulating the collapse of the colonial system.

Besides colonies there are semi-colonial, underdeveloped countries, where anti-national puppet dictatorial regimes, backed up by the foreign armed force, are in power. In a disarmed world the millions in the semi-colonies will gain new opportunities for eliminating the pro-imperialist regimes and establishing genuinely national states reflecting the will and aspirations of the peoples.

The logic of general and complete disarmament will also lead to the abrogation of unequal military and political treaties and the liquidation of aggressive military blocs which now enmesh in their nets a number of politically independent countries of Asia, Africa and Latin America. In a world gripped by the arms race and tension such agreements and blocs are used by modern monopoly capital for its colonial expansion in new camouflaged forms.

The peoples of the young sovereign states pursuing an independent national policy are also interested in the early eradication of all vestiges of colonialism. They know that the freedom they have won is not secure so long as imperialism keeps its strong points and military bases in neighbouring countries or in their territories. In a world where the monopolies are still seeking to resolve international issues by force of arms, where mushroom-shaped clouds constantly threaten mankind with another world war, they have no guarantee against intervention by the colonialists, against the restoration of the colonial system in some form or another. Freedom and peace are interconnected—this was the conclusion drawn by the Bandung Conference, and it has been corroborated by the entire record of post-war developments.

For the peoples of the underdeveloped countries political independence is not an aim in itself, but a necessary prerequisite for eliminating the dire economic and social aftermath of prolonged colonial rule. To understand the complexity and the tremendous difficulties of this task we must bear in mind the following facts. The entire large group of unindustrialised countries, inhabited by more than two-thirds of the population in the non-Socialist world, now produces *per capita* only about one-twentieth of the manufactured goods, including less than one-fortieth of the basic metals and about one-sixtieth of the machinery and equipment, produced by the industrially developed capitalist countries.

Agriculture in the underdeveloped countries, which as a rule contributes more than half of their national income, is based on hand labour and primitive implements. Labour productivity in agriculture is but a fraction of that in the advanced countries. The result is that *per capita* national income in the backward countries is only 10–11 per cent of that in the industrial capitalist states.

Social and epidemic diseases and starvation are still rampant in the overwhelming majority of colonial and former colonial countries, and their medical and social services are very meagre. The average life span is much lower than in the developed states, and child mortality per 1,000 of population is four to five times higher.

In the period when imperialism and colonialism ruled undivided over the whole world economic growth rates in the colonies hardly kept pace with the increase in population, and in some cases even lagged behind it. The post-war break-up of the colonial system has accelerated the economic advance of many liberated countries, but on the whole it is still slow. In the last decade, *per capita* real income in all underdeveloped countries rose on the average less than

2 per cent annually. Should these rates be preserved, the eradication of colonialism's most terrible legacy—the vast difference in economic development levels between countries—might persist for many, many decades to come. But mankind has no right to tolerate such a situation.

The peoples not only of these countries but of all other countries without exception are interested in accelerating the growth of their productive forces. There can be no lasting peace and security on earth, mankind will not be able to advance swiftly and in all fields if the vast gap in living standards of different countries remains for several generations, if the economic and social aftermath of colonialism is not eliminated in a brief historical period, if the staggering poverty of the masses in the underdeveloped countries plundered by colonialism is not swiftly wiped out.

Has human society the material requisites for solving, in the foreseeable future, the very complex socio-economic problems confronting the underdeveloped regions? The record of some countries, which have won real independence, the sweeping scientific and technical revolution now under way and the discovery of new, practically unlimited sources of power, show that such possibilities exist. But to exploit them to the maximum people need above all a lasting and durable peace based on general and complete disarmament.

Mankind is now spending colossal sums on the arms race, equivalent to at least two-thirds and, according to some estimates, to the entire national income of all the underdeveloped countries combined. This means that every year a quantity of material values equal to that created by the labour of more than 1,000 million people in these countries is wasted on military purposes. No less striking is the comparison between military expenditure and capital investments in the economy of these countries. The Economic and Social Consequences of Disarmament report points out that "despite the inadequacies of the available statistics it appears that the world's military expenditures far exceed the combined gross investment expenditures of the less developed areas; they are probably at least five times as large and may be much greater". Consequently, the employment of even a part of these funds for advancing the backward economy of the former colonial and dependent countries would within a few years send their economic and cultural development rates soaring upwards and would considerably improve the living conditions of their peoples.

In a disarmed world the financial and material resources which the underdeveloped countries themselves are now compelled to assign for military purposes could be *fully* used for these lofty aims. At present their military budgets, although relatively small as compared with the most developed countries, make up the sizable sum of more than $6,000 million annually.

This sum is nearly twice as large as the average annual influx of foreign funds to the underdeveloped countries in the form of net subsidies and net long-term loans. The proportion of military budgets to basic investments by national capital in most underdeveloped countries, as in most other countries, has been above 10 per cent in recent years. According to data in the U.N. report, in 1957–1959 this share amounted on the average to 12.3 per cent in the Sudan, 22.4 per cent in Brazil, 25.6 per cent in Chile, 17.6 per cent in Ecuador, 13.2 per cent in Peru, 26.3 per cent in the Malayan Federation, 24.4 per cent in Pakistan, etc.

V. STRIGACHEV: I can give this example. To ensure a 2 per cent increase in *per capita* national income in the underdeveloped countries (it is now less than 2 per cent) additional capital investments of about $7,000 million are needed every year. This sum, as V. Rymalov pointed out, is roughly equal to the present military expenditure of the underdeveloped countries, and can therefore largely be obtained from internal resources after general and complete disarmament.

V. RYMALOV: Many other economic factors directly bound up with disarmament will also become extremely important in mobilising the internal resources of the underdeveloped countries for carrying out economic development programmes. Once international tension eases off, the quite substantial amount of foreign exchange now spent by these countries for the purchase abroad of arms and ammunition could be used chiefly for importing industrial plant and other means of production. In addition to these newly released financial resources, the switching over to peaceful production of war industry plants, which have been built up fairly rapidly in some Asian and Latin American countries in the last few years, would enable them to increase the output of capital equipment and the other manufactured goods they need.

Moreover, demobilisation will make it possible to employ labour resources in social production more rationally, especially in view of the great shortage of skilled labour in the underdeveloped countries.

A substantial part of their technicians and other specialists is now claimed by the army.

I could mention several other factors to illustrate the favourable effect disarmament would immediately have on the economy of backward countries. Their impact can hardly be overstated, but the normalisation of international economic relations once the unequal economic ties existing between developed and underdeveloped countries are abolished, will be especially important. This inequality which arose during the period of domination of the world economy by colonialism and imperialism, stills prevails in the world capitalist economy today. In a world without arms and wars, where there will be only a free community of states enjoying full national sovereignty and political independence, inevitably the principles of equal co-operation, mutual assistance and mutual benefit in economic relations between countries irrespective of their political and social system will eventually prevail.

An idea of the benefits awaiting the underdeveloped countries in a disarmed world, after the last vestiges of colonialism in the world economy have been eliminated, is given by data which N. S. Khrushchev brought forward in his report on the C.P.S.U. Programme at the 22nd Congress. At present unequal relations between countries enable the monopolies of the United States and the other Western Powers to extract $20,000 million annually from the underdeveloped countries.

An end to this plunder will most certainly mean a loss for the monopolies, but, on the other hand, it will be a gain for the peoples. The use of these funds for industrialisation and the advance of agriculture in the backward countries will make it much easier to solve a vital problem for mankind, namely, to raise swiftly the living standards of their population of more than 1,000 million. This will be the starting point for quickly expanding their home markets and, consequently, the world market as a whole, and this will create additional favourable conditions for the further advance of productive forces in both the underdeveloped and industrialised countries.

The wide gap in social and economic development can be bridged only through the widest introduction of the latest achievements of science and technology in the economy of the backward countries, but there are serious obstacles to acquiring everything of value created by man's genius. The reason is not only that the arms race with all its consequences diverts huge material and technical resources of the developed states which could be used to speed up the economic advance of the former colonies and dependent countries. It is also necessary to remove once and for all the danger of predatory wars and to create everywhere a climate of mutual confidence among nations, in which aid could not be used to the detriment of the recipient countries.

Lenin pointed out that "only great concern for the interests of different countries removes grounds for conflicts, removes mutual suspicion, removes apprehension of any intrigue and creates that confidence, particularly among workers and peasants who speak different languages, without which both peaceful relations among nations and any successful development of everything of value in modern civilisation is absolutely impossible".

General and complete disarmament is the decisive condition for the creation of this kind of international climate. It will open up boundless horizons for the strengthening of friendly scientific, technical, and economic co-operation among the peoples, so needed by the countries liberated from colonial bondage. The opportunities available to the industrial states for passing on their scientific and technical know-how and giving aid to these countries will increase immeasurably in a disarmed world. Demobilisation and the discontinuation of weapons production will release many highly qualified specialists in the industrialised countries who will be able to apply their experience and knowledge to help the peoples of the underdeveloped countries attain a better future.

At the same time industry in the developed countries, freed from the burden of war production, will be able to provide the technically backward countries with the latest machinery, equipment and other goods on an unprecedented scale. The financial basis for assistance will increase many times over.

The principal industrial states are now spending approximately $100,000 million annually for war purposes. If at least a third of these funds now being used unproductively were used to advance the economically underdeveloped countries (this is perfectly feasible since the peoples are interested in consolidating world peace and accelerating the growth of productive forces throughout the world), the general resources for aid to these countries would reach some $35,000 million or $40,000 million annually.

V. STRIGACHEV: Additional annual investments in the economy, health services, housing and the construction of cultural establishments in the underdeveloped countries have to be of the order of $20,000 million–$40,000 million so as to ensure a 4–6 per cent annual growth of the *per capita* national income, thus enabling their peoples to overtake the developed states as regards living standards in a historically brief period, within a few decades. This is the sum named by V. Rymalov. As far as the Western world is concerned, this would merely represent the returning of a negligible part of their unpaid debt to the peoples of the underdeveloped countries.

By the way, *disarmament and the consequent development of the economically backward countries would be of benefit for the capitalist states as well, because it would stimulate capital construction.*

Paul Hoffman, well-known American economist, has estimated that "if with the help of the United States and other advanced countries, underdeveloped countries reached our proposed goal of increasing their annual *per capita* income by 25 per cent over the period 1961–1970 [or 2.5 per cent annually—V.S.] it would provide the United States with $110,000 million worth of business over the decade ahead. This would bring the United States exports to these countries to the level of $14,000 million in the year 1970, or more than double the total of our exports to these same areas in 1958".

F. Baade, a West German economist, said: "If *armaments are sharply reduced on a world-wide scale* and the Great Powers agree to assign part of the money thus saved to an international Fund to accelerate the building up of industry in the underdeveloped countries, this would be a *major contribution to a prolonged high level of activity* in the manufacture of capital equipment in the old industrial countries. . . ." Baade assumes in particular that disarmament and the resultant growth of public construction and aid to underdeveloped countries would increase by 1975 the production of steel in the countries of Europe and North America by 50 per cent, necessitating the expansion of the iron and steel industry.

I can give a very vivid example of this. To raise agriculture to what would be regarded as a high level in the capitalist world (one tractor per 40 hectares of land and 30 kilogrammes of fertiliser per hectare), the underdeveloped countries need an addition 15 million tractors and 17 million tons of mineral fertiliser annually (in 1957–1958 the entire capitalist world had 8.5 million tractors and consumed 19.5 million tons of mineral fertiliser). It is clear that to meet such needs, representing a huge capital outlay, large industrial investments would be required in all countries.

M. GORYAINOV: We have every ground for believing that general and complete disarmament will open up truly fantastic prospects before the whole of mankind.

Modern culture, industry, science and technology have been built up by the efforts of many and many generations. What they have created is tremendous. But the present generation has been destined by history to make the most significant changes in the life of human society.

It was only five years ago that the Soviet people launched the first sputnik. A little over a year ago a Soviet citizen made the first space flight, with others following in his wake. No doubt, man will land on the moon in the next few years and will visit other planets of the solar system within the lifetime of the present generation.

The present generation can also be proud of achievements in material production. In the last 40 years power capacity per worker throughout the world has increased more than three times (in the previous 40 years this process was nearly three times slower in a country such as the United States). The increase in power capacity has been particularly rapid in the Soviet Union.

The development of transport and communications has changed all conception of the scale of time and space. The globe has seemed to shrink greatly, and the peoples have drawn much nearer to each other.

Scientists have discovered ways of releasing nuclear energy, which is laying the new foundations of the power industry of the future. The surveyed resources of nuclear fuels (uranium and thorium) contain immeasurably greater power than all known stocks of coal, oil and natural gas combined. Hundreds of thousands of tons of uranium-238 have already been mined and hundreds of tons of uranium-235 have been extracted. (The power contained in already mined uranium is sufficient to meet all the power requirements of mankind for several years.)

If the sources of power which mankind possesses are used rationally the peoples of the world will be saved from such disasters as starvation, poverty, epidemic diseases, illiteracy, etc., even in the lifetime of the present generation.

The material possibilities for this exist and are in the hands of the people.

At the present level of production in the technically advanced countries all man's requirements in food, clothing and shelter and all his spiritual requirements could be fully satisfied. Moreover, it would only be necessary to work not eight or seven, but five or six hours daily.

But that is not all. Speaking of the wealth existing in the world we should mention things which will become available over the next number of years. Eminent scientists are unanimous in their belief that science, technology and industry have created the preliminary conditions so that in the near future (to be more exact, in the next 15–20 years) people will be able to learn how to control thermonuclear reactions of the fusion of light elements. Control of these processes would multiply hundreds of times over existing power capacities and create new material foundations for life on earth, in which complete abundance of the good things of life will be limited only by reason.

Mankind's immediate future within the next few decades—many of us will live in it—will be a world of marvellous achievements, a world of creative thought and joyous labour for every person, a world of universal happiness.

G. POKROVSKY: I think we need hardly speak in terms of decades ahead. It seems to me that the exceptional successes won in recent years in the study of space enable us even now to speak of the possibility of, for example, international co-operation in the further exploration of space and, moreover, *convincingly prove the benefits of such co-operation for all states without exception.*

We all know that the Soviet Union and the United States have invested immense resources and funds in the exploration of space in recent years and have registered substantial achievements. Today it is not difficult to outline definite trends for the successful development of co-operation between our two countries. After John Glenn's flight three times round the earth, following the flights of Yury Gagarin and Herman Titov, N. S. Khrushchev proposed to President Kennedy a pooling of the efforts of Soviet and American scientists in further space exploration for peace and progress.

He put forward, as an example, two tasks which could become the subject of joint exploration and research in the near future. The first is the establishment of a system of automatic earth satellites to ensure world-wide shortwave radio communication and in particular world-wide television.

The second task is the launching of sputniks for meteorological purposes, specifically, for effecting a great improvement in long-term weather forecasting.

How would these ideas work out in practice? I should like to discuss this point today. Since, naturally, I cannot go into a detailed discussion of technical problems, I will deal only with the fundamental aspects of the matter.

It was established long ago that shortwave radio relay lines are the most suitable for radio communication and can ensure all kinds of communication, from the telephone to television. These lines are almost free from interference and can work faultlessly.

But high towers with exactly pointed reflectors are needed for carrying these lines. The towers must be erected at distances of not more than 100 kilometres and must be no less than 100 metres high. This means that radio relay communication can be established only on land since it cannot be established across oceans by ordinary means.

High-frequency electric oscillations can also be transmitted along special cables, but in this case special amplifying stations have to be built at intervals of approximately 10 kilometres, making this type of communication even less widely applicable and more costly.

The situation would be entirely different if high towers were to be replaced by a system of earth satellites. For example, three sputniks flying at an altitude of about 36,000 kilometres above the earth would be sufficient to ensure world-wide television communication (except for relatively small areas around the Poles). By using radio shortwave reflectors mounted on sputniks it will be possible to make all forms of radio relay communication reliable and precise. Moreover, some other tasks could also be accomplished, namely, improvement and extension of international telephone, telegraph and telephoto communication, improvement of sea and aerial navigation, etc.

These measures will extend international ties and enable people in different countries throughout the world to get to know each other better. Moreover, all world radio communication and television will become much cheaper and more profitable. I estimate that the direct gain could reach nearly 10,000 million rubles annually.

We may assume that a system of communication via sputniks set up for the good of all countries and peoples will be profitable from the very outset, not to mention the benefits which will swiftly multiply as the system develops.

Space communication facilities, clearly, cannot serve *only one* state: by their very nature they are, so to say, world-wide, global. At the same time they become more and more useful to the extent to which international co-operation becomes more widespread and complete.

The problems connected with the use of sputniks for long-term weather forecasting are more intricate, but still more intriguing.

In this science unfortunately not everything is well under control. It is still impossible to predict the weather for the entire crop period exactly enough to be able to plan agricultural work with scientific accuracy and to determine the size of the future crop. As a result, many countries have suffered and are suffering huge losses; in the underdeveloped countries every crop failure and other calamity due to the whims of the weather—floods, frosts, drought—as a rule cause epidemics, famine and a huge death toll.

It may be assumed—with a fair degree of probability—that better long-term weather forecasts which would make it possible to predict, at least in half the cases, the conditions of the crop and natural calamities would give mankind a saving of not less than $100,000 million annually.

What is needed to make this possible?

For an answer to this question we should recall that various solar radiations which do not reach the surface of the earth but are absorbed in the upper layers of the atmosphere play an essential part in the life of the atmosphere. Of no less significance is heat radiation from the earth into outer space, which can conveniently be observed outside the atmosphere, in outer space.

Data about these radiations and also a picture of the cloud positions distinctly seen from outer space, are very necessary for a complete idea of the processes which take place in the atmosphere and determine the weather. That is why a system of meteorological sputniks for obtaining better basic weather information can greatly extend the possibilities of more precise long-term weather forecasting. The outlays for setting up and operating such a system will of course be considerable, but the benefits to agriculture, transport and other spheres of human endeavour from improved weather forecasts would most likely be tens of times greater than expenditure.

Deeper study of weather-making phenomena will enable man not only to predict but also to control the weather in future. The benefit to mankind is something we cannot even imagine today.

I have mentioned only two examples of the possible use of space for peaceful purposes in the interests of all countries. Of course, the list of examples could be continued *ad infinitum*. But that is not the main thing. The main thing is that mankind *in exploring space has boundless opportunities to solve through joint effort problems of practical benefit.*

There have, of course, already been several instances in international relations when international co-operation has been organised, despite differences in political systems, and this has yielded important practical results.

We can recall, for example, the First International Geophysical Year (1957–1958), the joint study of the Antarctic by expeditions coming from many countries, the agreement between the Soviet Union and France on the study of magneto-electrical phenomena in the upper layers of the atmosphere (the building of twin observatories at Yaransk in the Soviet Union and on Kerguelen Island (France), the International Quiet Sun Year, etc.

This experience shows that life itself impels people to closer and ever wider co-operation: the sooner and the more completely people understand this objective law of our age, the bigger the benefits all the nations will reap, and in the first place, those which display the greatest initiative and resourcefulness in this matter. Attempts such as the United States is making at the present time, to turn the Cosmos into an area for the arms contest, will not only deprive mankind of these benefits but will make more terrible the threat hanging over them.

M. GORYAINOV: Against the background of these staggering prospects, war stands out in all its stark madness.

We may recall that in the last two world wars, imposed on mankind by the imperialists, more than 60 million people were killed and over 100 million were wounded and crippled. Thousands of towns and scores of thousands of villages were destroyed. Over 100 million people were twice sent to the battlefields and about 500 million were made to work for war.

The cost of the two world wars is estimated at nearly $2,000,000 million. How vast this sum is can be seen from the fact that all the national wealth of the United States of America by the end of the Second World War was estimated at $600,000 million.

The wealth of North and South America is estimated at about $1,000,000 million, and of the entire capitalist world at $2,000,000–$2,500,000 million. These rough calculations show that mankind paid for the two world wars unleashed by imperialism with a toll of 60 million dead and 100 million wounded and maimed, and with nearly half of the material values the world possessed.

From 2 to 3.5 per cent of the world's population were killed or maimed and nearly 50 per cent of the world's wealth was consumed in the flames of war—this is the price mankind has already had to pay for the two world wars.

The present-day arms race and the cold war are in the same category as the two world wars. Total expenditure by all the countries on the arms race in the post-war period is close to $1,000,000 million. This sum (in comparable prices) is almost three times greater than the total cost of the First World War. Within the next several years, if cold war expenditure continues to rise at the present rates (it already exceeds $120,000 million annually), the arms race will have cost as much as the Second World War.

In the post-war years direct military expenditure in the United States reached $630,000 million and, together with indirect outlays, $842,000 million.

A comparison of the present cost of war preparations with those before the First and Second World wars is highly instructive.

In 1913, Britain, France, Germany, the United States and Italy spent altogether only $1,100 million to $1,200 million for military purposes. In 1933–1934 the same countries were already spending about $3,000 million and in 1938–1939 some $8,500 million to $10,000 million. Today the arms race is much more expensive: it swallows up over 10 per cent of the labour resources of the world. The arms race has resulted in the building up of a war machine, estimated now at $320,000 million to $350,000 million. This is greater than the cost of the First World War. The cost of the United States war machine is estimated at $160,000 million to $170,000 million.

Financial outlays, however, are only one aspect of the matter. With the invention of nuclear weapons, the means of destruction have become tens of thousands of times more powerful and the "technology" of destruction and murder, hundreds of times cheaper. The destructive potential of stockpiled nuclear warheads (calculated on the basis of data published in the American and British press), expressed in terms of TNT, is 15,000–20,000 times greater than the destructive power of all the explosives used during the Second World War. But even this is not all. To destruction potential should be added the radio-active potential which acts on living nature for a long period, at times over many years.

Stockpiles of nuclear explosives, it has been calculated, are sufficient to contaminate the entire surface of the globe and the adjacent layers of the atmosphere with a high concentration of radioactive substances. Between 50–60 per cent of the land surface of our planet would contain concentrations which after a certain brief period could cause the death of people. On the remaining part of our planet people would get a big radiation dose.

Attention should be drawn to the following: in pre-nuclear wars when people were chiefly the victims of aimed fire, human losses amounted to very low percentages of the world population, while material losses were relatively 20–25 times higher. Today a single nuclear explosion can cause destruction over hundreds and thousands of square kilometres and contaminate people with radio-active fallout over tens of thousands of square kilometres. This would sharply raise human losses both in absolute and relative terms.

One more tragic feature distinguishes the modern war machine from its pre-nuclear forerunner. Formerly, in peacetime armed forces were merely a burden on the economy. Present-day armies can spread death without fighting, in peacetime too, owing to nuclear weapon tests.

It seems to me it is easier in the light of all this, to answer the question: what will disarmament and the banishing of war give mankind?

The most important thing is that the world will be rid of the nightmare of nuclear-missile war. In time the atmosphere will be cleared of radioactive particles harmful to health. The peoples will have the possibility of using colossal sums of money for improving living conditions, advancing culture, for progress and the mastery of the secrets of the Cosmos. Peace on earth is the keystone for mankind's advance to a better life in the near future. In conclusion I want to stress that all peoples must get a better understanding of the full gravity of the menace of a nuclear-missile catastrophe hanging over the world so as to remove it forever.

N. TALENSKY: I should like to draw your attention to an urgent problem which has not however been sufficiently studied—the destruction of armaments and other war material as such and their conversion to peaceful uses.

General and complete disarmament is not for us a propaganda slogan, as some of our adversaries allege, but a real policy. We shall strive for disarmament despite the resistance of the forces of imperialism and shall not give up until we achieve complete success. That is why in spite of all the obstacles raised by the imperialist

Powers in the way of general and complete disarmament, we consider it necessary to work out in detail all aspects of this problem.

The Soviet Draft Treaty on General and Complete Disarmament is proof of our thorough approach. The problem of the destruction of weapons and military equipment requires a similar degree of thoroughness, since it is an extremely complicated process. Hundreds and thousands of rockets of different types designed for various purposes, huge stocks of rocket fuel and fissionable materials for the manufacture of nuclear weapons, thousands of nuclear bombs, rocket warheads and missiles will have to be destroyed. The most diverse types of electronic equipment employed in servicing nuclear weapons and anti-nuclear devices will also be liable for destruction as such.

The destruction of conventional armaments will necessitate an even greater volume of work: tens of thousands of tanks and self-propelled guns, military aircraft and helicopters, hundreds of thousands of machine-guns, millions of rifles and submachine-guns, ordnance pieces of various calibres intended for different purposes and literally mountains of munition for them, are due for destruction.

This, I repeat, would be a complicated process in which political, strategic, military-technical and economic aspects would be closely inter-connected. Therefore, since the main component of the disarmament problem is a basic treaty on general and complete disarmament under strict international control, the aspect of armaments destruction should also be kept in mind. In my opinion, it would be useful even now to undertake a serious study of the practical problem of destroying weapons and other war matériel. World and national public opinion would be of great assistance in this respect to both international disarmament bodies and national Governments.

Public participation in the preparation and implementation of a treaty on general and complete disarmament would be extremely useful and even essential, inasmuch as aggressive circles opposed to disarmament even after the signing of a treaty would try on every occasion to hamper its implementation, and to this end would above all take advantage of the complexity of the disarmament process.

Although I cannot even hope to give an exhaustive definition of the problem of destroying armaments and military equipment after the conclusion of a disarmament treaty, I will try to outline some of the basic principles and features of this process. Politically, it should be completely in accord with the treaty, and failure to observe the treaty as a whole or in part should be made absolutely impossible. Strict international control and the efficient working of the control apparatus supplemented by a broad system of public control, on a world-wide and national scale, would serve as a sufficiently reliable guarantee in this respect.

From the strategic and military-technical point of view, armaments destruction process should proceed in such a way that all measures would correspond strictly to the principle of symmetry and mutual balance. At no stage of the disarmament process should any participant be given strategic or military-technical advantages over any other participant; the relation of forces that exist at the time of signing a treaty on general and complete disarmament, and their stability, should not be disturbed.

The danger of an aggressive war in any form should be consistently and steadily lessened until it is reduced to nil. In the light of this principle, the only system of disarmament to have an absolute advantage over all others is that which is based on the destruction, in the very first stage, of the most dangerous armaments and above all the means of nuclear attack: all types of delivery vehicles and military bases which are centres for nuclear attack and aggression. Such a system of disarmament is envisaged in the plan proposed by the Soviet Government.

The political, strategic and military-technical principles underlying the process of implementing a disarmament treaty should be the same for all its signatories. In regard to the economic aspect, prominence should be given to one common principle: in destroying arms and military equipment as such, the possibility of reconverting them to military use should in no circumstances be preserved. Consequently, those types which are designed for delivering a blow should be made incapable of doing so, i.e., they should be either physically destroyed or rendered absolutely unsuitable for war purposes.

War matériel which can be employed without any danger of their being used for military purposes could be transferred to appropriate organisations or persons for peaceful uses. In this case it would become possible in the very process of disarmament to render substantial assistance to underdeveloped countries by turning over to them, say, motor and air transport facilities, various means of communications and so on.

Since war matériel is the product of people's labour and costs great sums of money, it is desirable to regear it as much as possible for use in the national economy. This principle will be most fully and rationally applied in the Socialist countries and in countries where the state controls, even if only partially, the economy. The capitalist countries would perhaps do the same as they did after the last war, when enormous stocks of materials suitable for peaceful purposes were physically destroyed.

In order to express in concrete terms the process of liquidating separate categories of armaments and military equipment, I shall pick out the following aspects. All delivery vehicles should in principle be completely destroyed, but in view of the fact that, as disarmament proceeds, the nature of inter-state relations will radically change and today's tension will give place to peaceful co-existence and broad co-operation, a certain number could be retained for peaceful, mainly scientific, uses under international control.

It is quite possible that a considerable number of powerful intercontinental missiles would be retained, under control, for space exploration conducted on a national and international scale. Disarmament would probably create immediate favourable conditions for linking up meteorological services throughout the world, as Maj.-Gen. Pokrovsky has said. Naturally, the transfer of various kinds of rockets, which can easily be adjusted to peaceful pursuits, to this service will be very useful. The meteorological service will probably take over a considerable proportion of ground installations for the launching of rockets and their control in flight.

The existing rocket stockpiles and launching ramps would provide as ample opportunity for research into the use of passenger and freight rockets and also for establishing a reliable international system of radio communication and television.

It would perhaps also be foolish to destroy nuclear submarines fitted with rockets. Released from military use, they could be widely employed for exploring seas and oceans and assisting the fishing industry, as is now being done by our own extremely popular *Severyanka*.

The forms of destruction of all other nuclear delivery vehicles should also make their use for military purposes absolutely impossible. As for their peaceful uses, these would be determined by considerations of an economic and technical nature. The ancient God of War which tries to prolong its combat life with the help of atomic missiles—atomic artillery—can find no peaceful application whatsoever and should therefore be consigned to the furnace.

Nuclear weapons could be most rationally done away with as

follows. Fissionable materials contained in bombs, rocket warheads, missiles and other devices should be extracted and together with reserve supplies form a country's special stock for peaceful uses, as envisaged by the Soviet Draft Treaty on General and Complete Disarmament. It goes without saying that these materials should be rendered useless for the direct re-creation of nuclear weapons and should be kept under proper control. These fissionable materials could serve as fuel for atomic power stations, sea-going ships of various descriptions and so on. They could also be widely used to help underdeveloped countries quickly establish electric power bases.

With their nuclear charge removed, it is hardly possible that bombs, warheads and missiles would find any peaceful application, and they should therefore be completely destroyed. All this should of course be done under strict control so as to make it impossible to violate treaty obligations.

The greater part of conventional armaments which cannot be employed for peaceful purposes should be melted down into metal for civilian uses. Supplies of explosives both in dumps and extracted from shells, mines and bombs can, to a certain extent, be used for peaceful work.

Other types of war matériel in the field or in depots, such as transport vehicles, and communication, construction, road-building and other equipment can be almost entirely used for peaceful purposes. A certain part of such equipment can also be turned over to the underdeveloped countries. For instance, the reserves of communication equipment in modern conventional armed forces are so great that it would be possible to meet the needs of many countries in them.

True, many types of this equipment would have to be readapted, but this would perhaps be preferable to destroying such expensive apparatus. As far as combatant and auxiliary warships are concerned, the following principle should be applied: all that could be used for peaceful purposes should be retained, while the rest would be subject to destruction. The same principle is applicable to chemical and bacteriological weapons.

These ideas are only an outline of the procedure for destroying weapons and other war matériel. To this should be added procedure for discontinuing military production and liquidating or regearing appropriate enterprises, factory shops, laboratories, etc. It should be emphasized that the basic principles of the process of eliminating all types of armaments have already been set out in the Soviet Draft Treaty on General and Complete Disarmament, and the document itself, the stages of, and procedure for, disarmament and the system of control set forth in it, provide the most favourable conditions for real disarmament and the creation of a world without arms and wars.

SH. SANAKOYEV: It seems to me we have had a useful meeting. We have of course made only an attempt at approaching a problem which is no longer an abstract idea: its solution is feasible in the near future. Clearly, the deliverance of mankind from arms and wars will bring great economic, political and social advantages. It will also be a moral victory for the peoples, since general and complete disarmament will at long last free them from the fear of nuclear death, which has nowadays become a serious hindrance to the development of civilisation.

However, it is important to realise that the way to a world without arms is by no means an easy one. This all-important problem of our age can be solved only through the stubborn and difficult struggle of millions of people in all countries and continents. The imperialist rulers talk a lot about peace; experience shows however that all their "peaceable" talk is nothing more than a fancy dress with which they try to deceive the peoples. That is why the struggle for peace is not so easy. In an effort to save the profits they are making out of the arms race, atomic hysteria and the cold war, the imperialists will no doubt do all they can to frustrate general and complete disarmament.

On the other hand, the existing relation of world forces is in favour of peace, progress and happiness. We have therefore every reason to hope that the struggle for peace will in the end be successful.